The Mamluks: The History and Legacy of the Established a Dynasty in Egypt

By Charles River Editors

A depiction of a Mamluk warrior

About Charles River Editors

Charles River Editors is a boutique digital publishing company, specializing in bringing history back to life with educational and engaging books on a wide range of topics. Keep up to date with our new and free offerings with this 5 second sign up on our weekly mailing list, and visit Our Kindle Author Page to see other recently published Kindle titles.

We make these books for you and always want to know our readers' opinions, so we encourage you to leave reviews and look forward to publishing new and exciting titles each week.

Introduction

A 15th century depiction of Mamluk lancers

Egypt in the 14th century was a glorious kingdom to behold. Spice merchants from Europe, Asia and Africa sailed up the Nile River to the great port city of Alexandria, carrying riches such as silk, jewels and spices. Cairo, the capital of Egypt, was the greatest city in the Islamic world, with a larger population and more wealth and splendor than any city in Europe. Cairo was a shining pinnacle of cosmopolitan splendor in the medieval world, and besides being a major trading hub, Cairo was famous for its scholars and intellectual class, offering countless academic opportunities for scholars across the Islamic world. The culture of Cairo was dynamic and famous for its wide range of intellectual debates on Islamic sciences and other academic fields, all of which far surpassed any contemporary city at the time. From across the Islamic world, scholars from all the major schools of thought were represented in Cairo. Spirited lectures occurred frequently in public squares and madrasas were often packed with patrons eagerly listening to readings by famed scholars. Cairo was a city filled with art, trade and knowledge.

However, there was another factor that made Cairo infamous. The city represented the last bastion of the Muslim world - a great Islamic caliphate, centered in Iraq, had once stretched from the edges of Central Asia to Spain, but invasions by outside enemies had mostly overrun this once mighty empire. The Mongol armies, pouring forth from their grasslands in Asia, had sacked Baghdad in 1258, destroying the caliphate and sending the Islamic world into a state of deep peril. Moreover, European crusaders had launched multiple invasions into Palestine and the Levant, threatening the very existence of the Muslim world.

Ultimately these foreign invaders were all stopped by one group: the Mamluks of Egypt, a group of warriors, slaves, and kings. Hailing from the Eurasian steppes, the Mamluks were not Arab, but ethnically Turkish, enslaved at a young age, and sold into military service in Egypt, where they underwent intense military training in Cairo. Thus, these Turkish warriors were utterly alien from the Arab populations they eventually ruled over in ethnicity, language and culture, but they were remarkably skilled in the mounted warfare styles of the nomadic tribes of the Eurasian grasslands and other aspects of medieval warfare. As a result, the Mamluks were some of the finest professional soldiers of their time, which they proved on multiple occasions through their brilliant military campaigns against the numerous enemies of Islamic Egypt. Critically, the Mamluks were one of the only groups to defeat the seemingly unstoppable Mongol hordes in open battle, potentially saving the Islamic world from annihilation. It could be argued that without the Mamluks, the Islamic world would have been completely destroyed, changing the course of history.

As the Mamluks took power in Egypt, they rapidly became the center of the Islamic world. Egypt's political system made it unique when compared to other parts of the Muslim world, and though the daily management of the kingdom required interactions between the foreign Mamluks and their Egyptian subjects, a vast degree of separation remained the law of the land. The Mamluks held a tight grip on political and military power (ordinary Egyptians were even forbidden to ride horses), and this system of recruitment from abroad and social isolation created an elite army loyal to the state and succeeded in barring the ruled people, even the sons of the Mamluks, from entering the ruling classes. Nothing symbolized this system better than the Citadel, a complex of mosques, offices, living quarters, stables, and palace that stood on a rocky prominence 250 feet above the city of Cairo. It was from the Citadel that the Mamluk sultan presided over his royal court and regiments of heavily armed cavalrymen, separated from the teeming masses of commoners who lived and worked on the streets below.

The Mamluks: The History and Legacy of the Medieval Slave Soldiers Who Established a Dynasty in Egypt examines what made the Mamluks so influential in Egypt, and how they took power. Along with pictures of important people, places, and events, you will learn about the Mamluks like never before.

The Mamluks: The History and Legacy of the Medieval Slave Soldiers Who Established a Dynasty in Egypt

About Charles River Editors

Introduction

    Egypt Before the Mamluks

    Islamic Military Slavery

    The Rise of the Mamluk Dynasty in Egypt

    The Wealth of Cairo

    The Mamluk "Family"

    The Royal Mamluk Army

    The Fall of the Mamluks

    Online Resources

    Bibliography

Free Books by Charles River Editors

Discounted Books by Charles River Editors

Egypt Before the Mamluks

Before the Mamluks established a dynasty in Egypt, the land was consolidated under the control of the legendary Saladin. According to legend, his father, a Kurdish mercenary named Najm ad-Din Ayyub (d. 1173), was forced into exile the night of Saladin's birth. Ayyub had gone against his own lord to give refuge to Zengi and his troops in 1132 after the murder of a rival Christian by his brother Shirkuh, a favor Zengi repaid six years later by giving Saladin's family asylum after Ayyub (who later lent his name to his son's dynasty) was exiled.

Ayyub fell out of favor in 1146 with Zengi's son, Nur ad-Din, when he surrendered the castle of Baalbeck while being attacked, but he was able to get back into Nur ad-Din's good graces by negotiating the surrender of Damascus to Nur ad-Din in 1154. Saladin therefore began his military career serving Zengi and Nur ad-Din under his father and his uncle Shirkuh. Therefore, while his fortunes came from the Zengids, his loyalties remained within his own family.

The Zengids and Ayyubids were very much a product of their period and of the wave of Turkish invaders from the previous century. The Seljuq Turks had arrived in the early 11th century from Central Asia by way of Persia and quickly conquered most of the area of Anatolia, the Levant and North Africa, leaving only a small area around Constantinople to the Byzantine Empire (which had previously held Jerusalem and the Levant until the early 7th century). But the Seljuqs were not a cohesive group, and they quickly fell apart into a loosely organized empire of squabbling nobles.

When the Byzantine Emperor subsequently sent envoys to the Pope in Rome asking for aid against the Seljuqs, it is most likely that he asked for and expected mercenaries. Pope Urban II, for his own reasons, decided the Byzantines needed a new thing – a crusade - instead. In one of the most famous events in the Catholic Church's history, Urban II exhorted the faithful to take up arms for the Holy Land and promised them remission of their sins if they died in battle. In November 1095, according to Fulcher of Chartres, the pope said, "I, or rather the Lord, beseech you as Christ's heralds to publish this everywhere and to pers-e all people of whatever rank, foot-soldiers and knights, poor and rich, to carry aid promptly to those Christians and to destroy that vile race from the lands of our friends. I say this to those who are present, it is meant also for those who are absent. Moreover, Christ commands it."

A disorganized European peasant army was easily destroyed by the Turks in 1096, but the army of nobles who followed later were better supplied and better trained. They took advantage of the unique circumstances of the Seljuqs' failing empire and the power vacuum left in its wake after the Seljuqs had replaced local Arab elites and traveled down through Anatolia. They took Jerusalem and large sections of the coastal Levant in 1099, two weeks before Urban II died in July of that year.

Pope Urban II

The Crusaders' descendants proceeded to fight a losing battle to keep the Holy Land for the next two centuries. At first, they were fairly successful due to the continuing power vacuum in the Muslim Near East. However, in the first decades of the 12th century, Imad ad-Din Zengi (no relation to Saladin's biographer) came to power and became determined to retake the Levant from the European invaders.

Zengi was born in 1085, and his early life was even more inauspicious than Saladin's, marked as it was by his father's execution as a traitor to his lord, Malik-Shah, who was nominal sultan of all the Seljuqs, when Zengi was 11. Zengi grew up in Mosul, a city on the Tigris River in what is now northern Iraq, and eventually became *atabeg* there in 1127. The following year, the *atabeg* of Damascus died, sparking a power struggle between Muslim and Christian leaders for the city. An *atabeg* was a Turkish governor (in this case, one ruling for the Sultan of Damascus in the Seljuq system). Zengi became ultimately independent, the Seljuq sultanate having fallen apart following the deaths of Malik-Shah and his highly competent vizier, Nizam al-Mulk, in 1092.

Perhaps inspired by his father, who had been the practical ruler of Syria before his execution, Zengi set out to expand his base from Mosul to Aleppo (which his father had ruled), Homs and the former Christian county of Edessa. The chronicler Ibn 'al-Adim quotes Zengi referring to himself as a "tyrant" and discusses the strong discipline that he maintained through fear over his troops. Zengi practiced a highly effective blend of ruthlessness, alliance and treachery, which did not make him unique among his rivals so much as he was simply better at it than others. He had become both hated and admired by the time of his assassination at the hands of a Frankish slave in 1146.

One problem with the Seljuq rulers, and one reason why their empire fell apart so quickly, was that they parceled out territories to their sons, so each ruler's fiefdom easily fell apart upon the death of a ruler. This was true of Zengi, as well. He left his Syrian territories to his second son,

Nur ad-Din, and his Iraq territories to his first-born son. The latter dynasty survived until the 13th century.

Nur ad-Din was more of a military leader than a game player in his father's mold. William of Tyre called Nur ad-Din a great enemy of Christian Palestine but also acknowledged him as a just and courteous enemy who became deeply religious after a major illness changed his outlook on life. Shortly after his father's death, Nur ad-Din made a change in his father's long-term strategy. He decided to conquer Egypt.

There were two reasons for this. One was that he and his older brother divided up their father's realm between them, so that the brother had Zengi's Iraq possessions and Nur ad-Din held Syria. This required that he make any future expansions to the south to avoid conflict with his brother, with whom he was on cordial terms. Second, the Crusaders had come to their own conclusions in the wake of the failure of the siege of Damascus during the Second Crusade and the final loss of the County of Edessa in the north. It became clear to them that they had little hope of making any progress in Syria. Therefore, they, too, needed to look south. Thus, both the Crusaders and Nur ad-Din now looked toward Egypt.

Egypt was a tempting prize, albeit not an easy one. The problem for the Crusaders was that they had a powerful Syria on their flank every time they tried to invade Egypt. The problem for Nur ad-Din, over and above any issue of religious conflict, was that uniting Egypt and Syria was almost impossible with the Crusader States lying in the way.

The Crusaders made their move first in the 1150s. The last Egyptian caliph, Al-Adid (1149-71), came to the throne in 1154, though the real power lay with his astute vizier, Shawar (d.1169). Shawar was in favor of allying with the Crusaders, which was not an especially popular position, and he had accrued a large fortune at the expense of the people, which was also not popular. However, he was good at manipulating the local emirs, who were characterized by crusader sources as weak and easily swayed. He also needed to do something to protect Egypt from her many enemies.

Allying with the Franks was not as odd a pairing as it might have seemed. In border regions between Islam and Christianity, like the Middle East and the Iberian Peninsula, during times when a victor was not clear and the battle went back and forth, even intense religious differences gave way to more regional and even clan or personal, differences. The gulf between the Shi'ite Fatimids, who had established their dynasty in the 9th century, and the Sunni Turkish Syrians, who had come almost as late to the scene as the Franks and were culturally almost as alien, was huge. Since the Franks had recently taken Egypt's last stronghold, Ascalon, this made them Egypt's *de facto* neighbors. It is unclear how much Shawar was aware of the ultimate goal of joining Syria with Egypt in the eyes of Syrian warlords like Nur ad-Din, but he was certainly aware that the Egyptian dynasty was as much at risk of being as completely destroyed by a Syrian Muslim invasion as by a Christian one. He therefore made the unpopular alliance with the relatively weaker and more over-stretched power.

The Syrians, for their part, were rough, violent, well-versed in war, and centered in their family loyalties. After Nur ad-Din sent his lieutenant Shirkuh (Saladin's uncle) to invade the country and break the Crusader hold, Shawar responded by expelling Shirkuh and accepting the Crusaders back, even brokering a treaty between the Franks and the young Caliph. It was not until 1169 that Shirkuh was able to invade and hold Egypt successfully, consolidating his power by executing Shawar. Shirkuh, however, did not live long to enjoy his success, for he died two months later.

19th century depiction of the victorious Saladin, by Gustave Doré.

It is at this point, at the age of 31, that Saladin was finally able to shine. Though Zengi's intervention in his family fortunes had greatly affected his life, he was still just an 8-year-old child when Zengi was assassinated. Therefore, his main lord had always been Nur ad-Din and his main influence had been his father and his uncle, Shirkuh, both of whom served Zengi and then Nur ad-Din.

Saladin had fought with his uncle on Shirkuh's Egyptian expeditions since 1164. The Ayyubids were clannish and close-knit, so Saladin's position in his uncle's army was literal nepotism, but this familial opportunism did not detract from his ability. M.C. Lyons and D.E.P Jackson, in their definitive biography, *Saladin: The Politics of the Holy War* (1982), note that Shirkuh picked Saladin as his *aide-de-camp* over his own sons, an indication of Shirkuh's recognition of his nephew's innate abilities. Shirkuh had a reputation (reported even by his enemies, like William of Tyre) for winning the loyalty of his men by living among them and sharing their hardships. Shirkuh was a coarse, short, fat man whose fierce temper that had gotten his family exiled from Tikrit, but he was also a shrewd general and a beloved military leader.

It is probably no coincidence that Saladin, too, acquired a reputation for living with his men and rousing their undying loyalty, though his appearance and personal habits were more moderate, like his nominal lord Nur ad-Din. No account of his life definitively explains what Saladin learned from Shirkuh, but a comparison of what contemporaries thought were their respective military strengths demonstrates that Saladin's experience, shrewdness, strategy, specific skills in exciting loyalty in his troops, work ethic, and even expeditious ruthlessness did not grow in a vacuum. He probably picked much of it up from observing his uncle over the six years he served him in Egypt.

For example, in one major battle with the Franks near Giza, Saladin was given charge of the right flank. He chose to put the baggage with his uncle in the middle (contemporary Muslim sources put Saladin in the middle), giving the impression of a weak center. Allowing a soft center so that the enemy can attack it and be surrounded by a pincer movement is an old tactic and very effective with a disciplined army that will hold together while being divided. Hannibal had famously used it to destroy a Roman army at the decisive Battle of Cannae over a thousand years earlier, and generals have been trying to use it with the same success ever since. In his own battle, Saladin successfully executed his part of the pincer and helped ensure the Franks were routed. This kind of experience would serve him well when his uncle was gone.

Shirkuh had ordered the assassination of Shawar, leaving a power vacuum upon his death. The young Caliph and his advisors chose Saladin as the new governor, according to Ibn al-Athir, because Saladin was perceived to be the weakest candidate and the least likely to be able to rally the Syrian emirs. Al-Wahrani claims that Saladin was chosen out of respect for his family's prowess, while Imad ad-Din claims that the Syrian faction forced Saladin on the Caliph. Whatever the reasons, Saladin did not simply walk into his position. He was forced to earn the loyalty of the emirs and make the Caliph's faction bend to his will, though he did so in part by making small concessions and using security matters (such as the Frankish invasion) to put down revolts and execute any emirs that opposed him.

There were many such revolts, perhaps exacerbated by the Syrians' practice of confiscating the Egyptian emirs' goods at will. According to Syrian chronicler Ibn Abi Tayy, "When a Turk saw an Egyptian, he took his clothes." Ibn Abi Tayy even accused the Syrians of evicting Egyptians from their houses without cause. Soon, there were riots in Cairo, the power center of the Caliphate. According to Abu Salih, Maqrizi and a letter by Saladin to Baghdad, Saladin was, as late as the summer of 1172, losing money to European merchants while facing sporadic-but-rising insurrection in a country in debt. Turning the situation around took far more than the nepotism that had put him at his uncle's side in the first place, and his success bode well and was a sign of his future greatness.

One of the first things Saladin did, aside from playing the Egyptian emirs against each other, was to consolidate his position by employing nepotism himself. He made the judicious appointment of trusted relatives to several important posts in his army and even got Nur ad-Din to send his father to Egypt. Unlike his later image as a patriot of Egypt (which was frequently invoked for propaganda purposes by the pan-Arab Nasser regime in the mid-20th century), Saladin did not choose to keep the old elite of Egyptian emirs, let alone the Caliphate, in place. Retaining the Caliphate would have been an option if he had chosen to remain a vassal to Nur ad-Din, but he was already moving away from that allegiance. Instead, he set out to destroy the old Egyptian Fatimid leadership and replace it completely with Syrians, encouraging his own men to have children and fathering four of his own by 1173. He did not father any children until he had passed the age of 30.

It is unknown at what point Saladin decided to defy Nur ad-Din, though he clearly engaged in a policy of expansion of power to balance out the problems going on in Egypt almost from the moment of Shirkuh's death. But it is entirely possible that he had no long-term plan at the time and only later became clear to him that expansion, especially east back into the Levant, would bring him into eventual and inevitable conflict with Nur ad-Din. Similarly, Nur ad-Din's motives for growing tired of waiting for Saladin are not entirely clear – or, at least, their origins are not clear. Some historians claimed that Nur ad-Din felt that Saladin was not sending him enough tribute from Egypt for the jihad back in Syria, but Imad ad-Din insists that Nur ad-Din did not want the money that Saladin later offered him.

Up to this point, Saladin had been no more a religious man than his uncle or Zengi, even according to his own biographers. However, the conquest of Egypt changed his outlook. Egypt was rich, fertile and chaotic enough to present him with many of the challenges that eventually made him a great general, yet also weak enough to provide him with an achievable conquest to retain. As part of this new awareness of his increased status in the world, he gave up wine and began to take the rules of Islam more seriously. This was a good thing, for he needed a clear head to deal with an assassination attempt later that year by the Egyptian faction. He then defeated a Crusader army near Damietta, before attacking Darum the following year.

In Egypt, Saladin was perhaps already trying to establish his legitimacy as a devout and just Muslim ruler who was replacing an older, corrupt elite that had fallen away from the true faith. Despite Saladin's later reputation for culture and gentility, fostered by his two biographers, even the faithful Imad ad-Din complained about his master's retainers, whom he referred to as "rough companions." Saladin therefore needed to create a basis for his right to rule that successfully counteracted both the hereditary legitimacy of those he overthrew and the rough lack of Arab culture in his own family. The intense loyalties within his own clan could only take him so far as long as they remained known solely as mercenaries and military governors.

Saladin now began to consolidate his power in Egypt, which included suppressing the local Shi'ite worship via the establishment of Sunni madrasas, pushing aside the minor Caliph (who conveniently died in 1171 and was replaced by a Sunni Abbassid Caliph after the Shi'ite emirs were massacred), and raising himself up as a virtual equal to his erstwhile lord, Nur ad-Din. All of these things were perfectly standard for an ambitious Seljuq leader and were signs that an astute leader like Nur ad-Din could not possibly miss.

This transfer of power to the new dynasty did not occur immediately. Any plans Saladin had of uniting the realms were put on hold as he engaged in a civil war with other claimants to Nur ad-Din's throne. His main difficulty arose from the fact that he had no legitimate basis for ruling in Syria, or for deposing the rightful Caliph and ruling Egypt for that matter. He was not related to Nur ad-Din, who had a living son and living adult brothers, as did Nur ad-Din's nominal lord in Baghdad. Saladin was only one of Nur ad-Din's mercenaries, and he had earned the distrust of Nur ad-Din and the Syrians concerning his devotion (or lack of it) to jihad by failing to provide financial assistance to Syria during the warring with the Christians. As such, Saladin had to pursue his goals in Syria through subterfuge and warfare.

Saladin's first break came in 1174, when the emir of Damascus reluctantly asked for his aid after being attacked by another former captain of Nur ad-Din, Gumushtigin of Aleppo. Gumushtigin had seized Nur ad-Din's heir, As-Salih, and tried to seize all of Nur ad-Din's territory. Saladin crossed the desert from Egypt with a select cavalry of 700. When he arrived in Damascus, he was welcomed as a liberator and immediately took over the castle there.

After leaving his brother to administer Damascus and taking the town of Hamah, Saladin then besieged Gumushtigin in Aleppo. Fearing Saladin's intentions, As-Salih himself begged the populace not to give in. The siege, as well as one made against the well-defended fortress at Homs, was thwarted by an attack by 13 Assassins, requested by Gumushtigin, and an opportunistic attack by the crusader Raymond III, Count of Tripoli (1140-87), who was at times both Saladin's enemy and ally. The Count of Tripoli was greatly respected in Europe, and

William of Tyre described him glowingly: "A man of slender build, extremely spare, of medium height and swarthy complexion. His hair was straight and rather dark in color. He had piercing eyes and carried his shoulders very erect. He was prompt and vigorous in action, gifted with equanimity and foresight, and temperate in his use of both food and drink, far more than the average man. He showed munificence towards strangers, but towards his own people he was not so lavish. He was fairly well-lettered, an accomplishment which he had acquired while a prisoner among the enemy, at the expense of much effort, aided greatly, however, by his natural keenness of mind. Like King [Amalric I], he eagerly sought the knowledge contained in written works. He was indefatigable in asking questions if there happened to be anyone present who in his opinion was capable of answering."

The siege had harmed Saladin's reputation in Syria because he had laid siege to a city where his former lord's son was taking refuge. This provided a propaganda boon for his Muslim enemies, but Saladin quickly raised the siege and used the crusader attack to show that he was defending the faith from the Franks. His fortunes in Syria began to change again when he was finally able to take Homs in March 1175.

His next rival was Saif ad-Din (d.1180), a nephew of Nur ad-Din, who marched against him in Hama with a superior army the following month. Worried, Saladin first tried to sue for terms, but was unable to win them. By judiciously deploying his forces on the high ground, he was able to use his battle-hardened soldiers (who had gained experienced from the civil war in Egypt) to crush the other army's superior numbers. This would not be the last time Saladin used this tactic, or that it would be successful. From this point onward, Saladin declared himself the ruler of Syria and eased as-Salih out. In Cairo, gold coins were minted with his new title: al-Malik an-Nasir Yusuf Ayyub, ala ghaya ("the King Strong to Aid, Joseph son of Job; exalted be the standard").

A picture of the Cairo Citadel, ordered constructed by Saladin in the 1170s

Saif ad-Din and Gumushtigin were not truly crushed, however, until 1176. Saladin defeated Saif ad-Din in battle in the spring and then made a truce with Gumushtigin and As-Salih in June, only slightly deterred by a solar eclipse he considered an omen and a nearly successful assassination attempt. During intense hand-to-hand fighting that drove Saladin's left flank back, Saladin personally led a charge that helped rout the Zengids, leaving Saladin in possession of the enemy's supplies. In a cunning move designed to build loyalty, he freed the Zengid prisoners of war and spread the loot around his army without taking anything of value himself.

Saladin spent the rest of the summer punishing the Assassins for the assassination attempt by laying waste to their territory. This had little effect, and he ultimately broke a truce with the Crusaders to ally with the Assassins instead. It was this alliance, and a battle at Tell Jezer in November, that perhaps explains Saladin's later hatred of the military orders, especially the Assassins' traditional enemies, the Knights Templar. He lost the battle because the Templars were able to reach his bodyguard and cut them down. Saladin escaped, but he had learned a lesson about these Frankish enemies who were every bit as hardened and disciplined as his men. He engaged in skirmishes with the Crusaders in 1178 and then took a major Templar castle, Jacob's Ford, at the end of August in 1179. In 1180, a drought forced him to agree to a peace with Baldwin IV, the last King of Jerusalem (1161-85).

During the infamous Third Crusade, Saladin essentially scored a strategic victory by retaining

Jerusalem, but the leader was too weary to savor the victory, and the damage Richard the Lionheart had done during his year in Palestine was just enough to revive the Crusader States. Saladin returned to Damascus and fell ill from a fever, which killed him on March 4, 1193. Shortly before his death, he drew up his will and gave away all of his possessions to the poor, retaining just a few pieces of gold and silver for himself. This was a traditionally humble death for a pious prince, and he was buried in a simple wooden box.

As soon as Saladin was buried, his great empire began to fall apart. He left behind 17 sons and various brothers who squabbled over his realm. In the traditional Turkish way, he had divided up leadership of the various areas among his relatives, which proved disastrous as his once large empire was quickly ripped asunder by fratricidal war. The competence of his sons ranged from the foolish (Al-Afdal, who only ruled Damascus for three years before being deposed) to the destructive (Al-Aziz Uthman, who took Egypt and tried to tear down the pyramids before dying in a hunting accident in 1198).

The much-reduced Ayyubid sultanate eventually fell to a brother, Al-Adil. He continued the line until the dynasty was destroyed by a combination of revolts among its slave soldiers, the Mamluks, and invasions by the Mongols in the 1250s. Since Al-Adil and his sons had little interest in continuing Saladin's attacks on the Crusaders, it would ultimately fall to the Mamluks to deal with the Crusader States in the late 13th century.

Despite his many successes, Saladin was rather quickly forgotten by his Muslim contemporaries after his death. Only 42 years after Saladin had captured Jerusalem, his nephew, Al-Kamil, was willing to give it back, and the Crusaders themselves were not especially willing to take it. His empire almost immediately fell apart, and the Christians returned to and rebuilt many of their former possessions. Within six decades, his dynasty would be replaced by the Mamluks, ensuring that Saladin's successes during his lifetime were largely ephemeral.

Islamic Military Slavery

Throughout history, the Islamic world's embrace of military slavery has been a relatively unique phenomenon, with no other region in the world possessing a system of military slavery that had the same impact, duration, and longevity. From the 9th century to the 19th century, stretching from Egypt to Central Asia and India, military slavery played a critical role in the Islamic armies, forming either the bulk of the fighting forces or proving instrumental as elite units. Military slaves often achieved great political influence, with some even becoming rulers of the state.

The origins of military slavery in the Islamic world can be connected to the Abbasid caliph Abu Ishaq Al-Mutasim, the third son of famed ruler Harun Al-Rashid. It was under the rule of Caliph Al-Mutasim that the system of military slavery came into widespread use in the Muslim armies.

A medieval depiction of Byzantine envoys visiting Abu Ishaq Al-Mutasim

However, the Islamic armies weren't always reliant on military slaves. During the first several centuries that Islam spread, the Muslim armies that poured forth from the Arabian Peninsula consisted mostly of tribal Arab warriors, most of whom were Bedouin nomads.[1] The Arab armies were well-led and had the advantage of facing enemies that were weakened and embroiled in chaos, most notably the Byzantine Empire and Sasanian Empire. Within a generation, this band of nomadic Arabs had succeeded in conquering Egypt, Syria, Iraq, Iran, most of the Caucasus, and North Africa. Even during this initial period of Arab conquest, non-Arab elements like the Persians had been integrated into the rapidly expanding Muslim armies. This inclusion was mainly due to the manpower demands of the Arab armies as they continued their wars of expansion.[2]

Under the Umayyad Caliphate (661-750), the Muslim armies were becoming increasingly professionalized and less reliant on its nomadic Arab warriors (although the army was still predominantly Arab). However, it was under the Abbasids, who overthrew the Umayyad Caliphate, that a fundamental change started to occur in the Muslim armies. Abu Muslim, the commander of the Abbasid revolutionary forces, started to register non-Arab troops in the dīwān (the payment list) by residence and not under tribal affiliation, as was the standard at the time.[3] This new act of military organization was the beginning of the eventual decline of the Arab tribal faction that had comprised the main body of caliphate armies up to that point in Islamic history.[4]

---

[1] Reuven Amitai, *The Mamluk Institution, or One Thousand Years of Military Slavery in the Islamic World* (Arming Slaves: From Classical Times to the Modern Age, 2006), 42.

[2] Amitai, 42.

[3] Amitai, 42.

[4] Amitai, 42.

In the beginning, the Abbasid armies composed of mixed Arab-Persian troops, with many of these men unable to speak Arabic. Abbasid armies also started to incorporate men from modern day Uzbekistan, known as Transoxania at the time, adding a Turkish element to its armies. The Turks were valued for their military prowess, which had been forged in constant battles on the Eurasian steppes. This began the trend of caliphate armies relying increasingly on men from the eastern edges of the empire, mainly the Turks.

The decline of the Arabs in the Muslim armies was gradual. Even during the Abbasid revolution (747-750) and the civil war (811-813), Arab tribesmen remained a critical component of the Muslim armies, but as time passed, the Arab component gradually lost its importance in the military. There were two main reasons for this development. Large portions of the Arab population had become urbanized, having settled in cities after the conquests and intermixing with the local non-Arab populations. Within decades, these formerly nomadic warriors began adopting a sedentary lifestyle and lost much of their desire and capacity for warfare. Second, among both the urban and remaining nomadic Arabs, they remained transfixed by tribal, political, or religious affiliations that often conflicted with the caliphate rulers, which meant that their loyalty was often fluid and could not be trusted.

The institution of mawali was another factor in the decline of the Arab Muslim armies. Originally defined as the clients of the Arab tribes, it was gradually instituted to apply to non-Arab converts of Islam before eventually being defined by all converts to Islam in the conquered nations.[5] By the Abbasid period, mawali was increasingly applied to refer to former prisoners of war and freed slaves. Often, these people came from the far edges of the empire, converted to Islam, and upon their release remained loyal to their patrons.

Most of these mawali were from the east, consisting of Persians, Transoxanians, and Turks, and these "imported" mawali represented the beginnings of the military slavery institution that the Mamluks would cultivate in the centuries to come. This institution would be built on isolation and alienation from the native population, combined with loyalty and dependence on a patron. These mawali converts were fanatically loyal at times, as demonstrated by a passage from the historian Al-Tabari when describing a group of mawali fighting for Muhammad ibn Yazid ibn Hatim al-Muhallabi , a senior officer in the civil war. When confronted with a losing battle, Muhammad told his mawali to flee, but the men refused, telling him, "'By God! If we do so, we would cause you great injustice. You have manumitted us from slavery, and elevated us from a humble position and raised us from poverty to riches. And after all that, how can we abandon you and leave you in such a state. Oh no! Instead of that we shall advance in front of you and die under your steed. May God curse this world and life altogether after your death."[6]

---

[5] Non-Arab Muslims. Initially referred to individuals captured and converted to Islam during the Muslim expansions in the Near East and Byzantine Empire. During the Umayyad dynasty (661-750) mawali were not given equal treatment compared to Arab Muslims (particularly taxes). This favored treatment of Arab Muslims was a problem since it breached the Quranic declaration of equality among all believers. Under the Abbasid dynasty (750-1258), these differences between Arab and non-Arab Muslims were dissolved.

This particular group of mawali eventually fought to the death alongside their patron and commander, demonstrating the zealous loyalty that could be fostered among these non-Arab soldiers.

This gradual use of foreign and non-Arab troops led to the creation of the Mamluks. Meaning "property" in Arabic, the first Mamluk military regiment was created by Abu Ishaq Al-Mutasim during the second decade of the 8th century under the reign of his brother, Caliph Al-Mamun.[7] During his reign, Al-Mamun had focused most of his efforts on creating a more centralized state. Under his brother Abu Ishaq, a new military institution began, one composed entirely of Turkish slaves. This fighting force of several thousand men was instrumental in helping Abu Ishaq gain the throne after the death of his brother while also becoming a pivotal fighting forces in military campaigns against the Byzantines.[8]

The development of the Mamluk system came about thanks to several factors. The existing mawali system, along with the addition of complete alienation from the local population, the patron-client relationship, and the recruitment of slave soldiers from the eastern frontiers of the Islamic world all factored into the continuation and acceleration of the Mamluk system. Furthermore, the inclusion of the Turks as a source of manpower was a major factor in the changing demographics of the Islamic armies. Even before the advent of the Mamluk system, Muslim rulers and commanders had been utilizing men hailing from the Eurasian steppes in Central Asia, and as warriors, the Turks possessed several important advantages. For one thing, they were pagans, so they could be legally enslaved within Islamic law. For another, there was a large preexisting population of Turks from which the Arabs could draw soldiers. Finally, and perhaps most importantly, the Turks were famous steppe warriors known for their prowess in archery, horsemanship, discipline, and fortitude in combat. Comparatively, the Turks were recent arrivals to the historical tradition of Eurasian steppe warrior culture which famously combined mobility with firepower.[9] This prowess in warfare was a direct result of the Turkish lifestyle as pastoral nomads who used domesticated horses. Throughout the entire grasslands of the Eurasian steppes, the nomadic horsemen in this region of the world were all potential cavalrymen, the most dangerous component of warfare in the ancient and medieval world. Groups of massed and highly mobile horse archers using composite bows were incredibly deadly in combat, and during the Middle Ages, nomads from the Eurasian steppes were the bane of every developed empire and kingdom in Asia and Europe. When these scattered tribal nomads reached critical mass and formed armies, they wreaked havoc almost everywhere they went.[10]

---

[6] Amitai, 44.
[7] Amitai, 44.
[8] Amitai, 44.
[9] The Huns that terrorized China and the Roman Empire also hailed from the Eurasian steppes, along with the Mongols. Amitai, 45.
[10] The invention of the stirrup for horse riders in the early modern period made the horse archers even more deadly. Amitai, 46.

A picture of Ottoman Mamluk heavy cavalry armor

Carl Vernet's painting of a Mamluk cavalryman charging

Contemporary Muslim sources during this time mostly praised the martial qualities of the Turks. The 10th century geographer Al-Istakhri wrote that "the Turks constituted [the caliph's] armies because of their superiority over the other races in prowess, valor, courage and intrepidity."[11] Al-Jahiz, a 9th century scholar from Baghdad, described the Turks as "became to Islam a source of reinforcement and an enormous army, and to the Caliphs a protection and a shelter and an invulnerable armour as well as an innermost garment worn under the upper garment."[12] Ibn Hawqal, a 10th century geographer, praised the Turks as "the most precious slaves are those arriving [in Khurasan] from the land of the Turks. There is no equal to the Turkish slaves among all the slaves of the earth."[13]

The process of Turkish military enslavement began at a very young age. Young Turks between the ages of 8-12 were enslaved and imported into the Islamic caliphate. Age was important for these Turkish military slaves, because if the boys were too young, they would not have been exposed to the steppe traditions of riding and archery, and it was vital that these military slaves possess some basic skills in steppe warfare before they received advanced training in Egypt. Once enslaved, they were converted to Islam, received basic religious education, and were exposed to intense military training that spanned several years, which made them highly skilled warriors. They were intentionally kept separate from the local population and remained entirely alien when it came to origins, language, and location. This isolation was designed to focus their loyalty upon their patrons.

---

[11] Amitai, 46.
[12] Amitai, 46.
[13] Amitai, 46.

Some of the most important individuals involved in the upbringing and training of the Mamluks were eunuchs. Royal eunuchs had long been an important component of the Islamic caliphal court, and due to the physical and physiological nature of the eunuchs, they were considered more trustworthy. The sultan placed these eunuchs as guardians of the royal harem, where they were also involved in the education of the children within the harem. This made the eunuchs ideal teachers for the young Mamluks and formalized a system that put a ready-made institution in place capable of both educating and developing military slaves. The eunuchs were critical in the rapid embrace of the Mamluk system by the caliphate. Regarding the often messy politics of the royal court, eunuchs played a key role as intermediaries between the Mamluks and the royal harem, which was of particular importance during times of political chaos.[14]

Of course, the Mamluk system depended on a consistent stream of slaves from the Eurasian steppes, and while some of these slaves had been enslaved during wars along the eastern frontiers of the caliphate, a more long-term and steady supply of recruits was necessary to maintain the numbers needed for the army. Thus, a supply system of independent traders supported by the royalty was created, and for this supply system to work, the caliphate needed the willing cooperation of the people that inhabited the steppes. The ensuing result was that steppe princes and tribal leaders willingly provided the caliphate with a steady supply of young male slaves, many of whom were sold into slavery after being captured during raids against rival tribal groups. Many families also sold their sons into the Mamluk system in difficult times (a common scenario during famines).[15] This concept was illustrated by the geographer Yaqut, who wrote in 1229, "If a man [of the Kimek tribe of Turkey] begets a son, he would bring up and provide for him and take care of him until he attains puberty. Then he would hand [his pubescent son] a bow and arrows and would drive him out of his abode telling him: 'fend for yourself!,' and he would treat him [henceforth] as a stranger and foreigner. There are amongst [the Kimek] those who sell their sons and daughters in order to cover their expenses."[16]

This enslavement system begets the question of why the caliphate refused to use the children of their Mamluk soldiers as potential recruits. After all, that would have saved the hassle of relying on an outside source of manpower for their military strength. But there were several reasons why this concept failed to work. Most notably, the sons of the Mamluks lacked the natural steppe warriors' qualities that had been ingrained in their fathers; growing up in the relative affluence of the urbanized capital, they were less hardy and did not have the natural exposure to the basic skills of horsemanship and archery. Also, unlike their foreign fathers, it was difficult to cut the sons of the Mamluks off from the local people and the various political and religious allegiances. Thus, in order to maintain this consistent alienation and loyalty to their patrons, a constant stream of fresh recruits from the steppe was needed to maintain the Mamluk military, even if it meant the sons of the Mamluks belonged to a very different social class than their fathers. Most

---

[14] Amitai, 47.
[15] Amitai, 48.
[16] Amitai, 48.

Mamluk sons entered larger society instead of living in isolation like their fathers, and a few Mamluk sons even became religious scholars. Some followed their father's footsteps and entered the army, but very few were a part of the prestigious units.

This system of military slavery was very successful during the reign of Al-Mutasim due to the soldiers' loyalty and high degree of military skill. These military slaves from the steppe were disciplined in mounted archery, a deadly combination before the advent of gunpowder, and within the first generation of their existence, the Mamluks had proven their worth on several military campaigns for the caliphate.

However, it was already evident that several serious flaws plagued the system even during this initial stage of its history. While the loyalty of the Mamluks to their patron was generally excellent, there were no assurances that this fealty would pass down to the ruler's sons or successor, because Mamluks often had economic and political interests that were in line with their patron but not with the patron's successors. A new ruler often had desires to further the interest of his own group of Mamluks, and in turn, these new groups of Mamluks sought to strengthen their patron's position since it also secured further power for themselves. As a result, there was constant potential for conflict among rival groups of Mamluks for political and economic control.

The Rise of the Mamluk Dynasty in Egypt

The rise of the Mamluk Dynasty in Egypt was tied directly to the chaos of the 11th century. Turkish warriors hailing from the Eurasian steppes had moved into the Middle East and seized power in various areas, filling the void left by the collapse of the Abbasid Caliphate in Baghdad. Turkish warlords, along with their alliances with the native Arab and Persian populations, were able to restore and rule over large swaths of the Middle East and Asia Minor, founding several military dynasties.

Many of these Turkish warriors were brought to Egypt to supplement the armies of the last Ayyubid sultan. Together these soldiers formed the elite Bahri regiment, serving as the sultan's bodyguards. On May 2, 1250, these troops staged a coup d'état in Cairo and took control, ousting the Ayyubid sultanate. For the next 50 years, the Bahri Mamluks (named for the fact that these slave soldiers were originally quartered on Bahr al-Nil, an island in the Nile river), cemented their power through a series of military campaigns against the Mongols and Christian Crusaders, marking the rise of the Mamluk Dynasty.

The Mamluks came to power during a tumultuous time. Islam was pressed on all sides, most importantly the Christians from the west and the Mongols from the east. The Crusaders had hoped to conquer Egypt, sensing weakness in the Islamic world after the destruction of the caliphate in Iraq, while the Mongols had reached the Middle East and wreaked havoc across vast swathes of the Arab empire, reducing the once mighty caliphate to a shadow of its former self.

Ultimately, the Mamluks stopped both of these threats. Compared to the Crusaders and their armies (with the exception of the Knights Templar and Knights Hospitaller) the Mamluks were a much more professional and disciplined military force. Many of the Mamluk troops during the Crusades were Kipchak slaves from Central Asia who had fled the Mongol hordes that were enveloping the continent at the time. Combining nomadic horse archery and classic Muslim tactics, the Mamluks defeated the Crusader States in the Levant and Cilicia in a series of campaigns.

The military prowess of the Mamluks was perfected under the rule of Sultan Baybars (1260-77). A man of humble origins, Baybars was of Turkic ethnicity. A tall and physically powerful man with pale blue eyes (his right eye had a prominent white spot), Baybars obtained his power due to his brilliant military mind, and under his command, he molded the Mamluk army into a highly efficient force that would maintain its preeminence in the region for the next hundred years.

A Turkish Kipchak hailing from southern Russia, he (like many Kipchaks) had been expelled from his homeland due to the Mongols.[17] Although some Kipchaks joined the Mongol armies, many of them were sold into slavery. Baybars was sold at Aleppo in Syria before eventually being sold again in Egypt, where he was sent to the Mamluk military school. Rising eventually to the rank of a commander in the Ayyubid army, Baybars achieved widespread military success before becoming sultan. He scored several victories against the Crusaders, defeating the forces of the Seventh Crusade under King Louis IX of France. The Frankish Crusaders arrived in the Levant with the goal of defeating the Ayyubids, but Baybars had other plans. At the crucial Battle of Mansoura, the Mamluks defeated the Franks, who proved no match for Baybar's Mamluks.

Baybars was an ambitious man who eventually ascended the throne of the Mamluk kingdom, and as sultan, Baybars continued his campaigns against the crusaders. He destroyed the remaining Crusader States in the Levant, capturing fortresses held by the Franks, Knights Templar, and Knights Hospitaller. These battles were mostly sieges, with the last siege ending in 1291 at Saint Jean d' Acre in Palestine. By 1375, the Mamluks would also conquer Christian Cilicia (Armenia), an ally of the Crusaders.

Perhaps the most pivotal campaign the Mamluks fought resulted in their victory against the Mongols in Syria. By the 1250s, Mongol hordes had already left a path of destruction across the Middle East. Hülegü, the grandson of Genghis Khan, had renewed a Mongol invasion in the Islamic world, and Baghdad fell in 1258, effectively ending the Abbasid caliphate. By 1260, Mongol armies had entered Syria and were poised on the very doorstep of Egypt. The Mongols were a terrifying force who struck fear into the hearts of everyone from China to Europe, and the

---

[17] Gérard Chaliand, *The Seljuks, the Mamluks, and the Crusades* (*A Global History of War: From Assyria to the Twenty-First Century*, et al., 1st ed., 2014), 135.

Mongol cavalrymen were notorious for their uncanny ability to cover enormous distances, sometimes advancing 70 miles a day. Expert horse archers, Mongol warriors could shoot deadly steel-tipped arrows from a distance of over 200 yards at full speed on their horses.[18]

The Ayyubid regime in Syria collapsed before the approaching Mongol armies, but in Cairo, there was defiance. Sultan Al-Muzaffar Qutuz greeted the Mongol emissary seeking his surrender with an aggressive statement - he beheaded the envoy and sent off a large army to face the Mongols. The commander of this force was Baybars, and he proved critical in defeating the seemingly unstoppable Mongols.

An army under the Mongol commander Kitbuqa had been dispatched into Syria and rapidly took the cities of Aleppo and Damascus (the city surrendered without fighting). Elements of the Mongol forces raided deep into Islamic lands, including Gaza, Jerusalem and into the areas of modern-day Jordan. But the Mamluks were prepared. They planned to face the Mongols in a decisive battle in Syria, and the Mamluks had a distinct advantage. Hülegü himself had withdrawn from the Middle East with a vast majority of his forces, taking a position in Azerbaijan, but he left behind Kitbuqa and his lone Mongol army in Syria. Kitbuqa was given specific instructions to keep an eye on the Franks and the Mamluks in Egypt.[19]

The Mamluks saw a chance to strike while the Mongols were weakened. Baybars led his Bahri Mamluks reinforced by the Ayyubid soldiers who had fled to Egypt from Syria, and this combined force marched towards Syria in July 1260, defeating the Mongols at Gaza. The Mamluks were also able to establish a neutrality pact with the Franks, who subsequently provided supplies.

With their flanks secure, the Mamluk forces moved into the Jezreel Valley in Syria. Kitbuqa and his Mongol forces soon arrived to confront the Mamluks, and the two armies faced each other at Ayn Jalut (The Well of Goliath). On September 3, 1260, the battle commenced, and it lasted for hours as the momentum went back and forth. The Mamluks eventually emerged victorious and pursued the fleeing Mongols, who abandoned Syria altogether. It was the decisive battle that checked the Mongol expansion into the Middle East; never again would the Mongols advance further.

---

[18] Anne Wolff, *The Mamluk Rulers of Egypt* (How Many Miles to Babylon?: Travels and Adventures to Egypt and Beyond, From 1300 to 1640, 1st ed., 2003), 15.
[19] Amitai, 58.

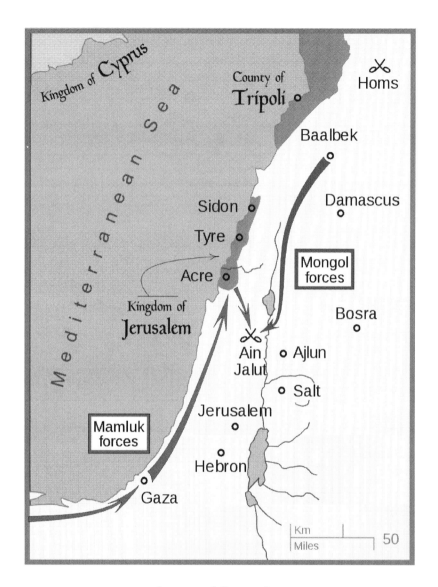

A map of the region

There were several reasons for the Mamluk victory against the Mongols at Ayn Jalut. The Mamluks enjoyed a numerical advantage as a result of the Mongol withdrawal under Hülegü. Elements of the Mongol army were also unreliable, especially the Syrian Muslim troops who had been pressed into the Mongol army against their will and fled the field when the tide turned. But the most important factor was that the Mamluks understood the Mongol way of warfare on an intimate level.[20] Being steppe warriors themselves, the Mamluks shared many similarities with the Mongols in warfare, and for a change, the Mongols encountered an enemy whose abilities and discipline were equal to their own. On this occasion, the Mamluks also had the advantage of fighting on familiar terrain.[21] In 1267, Syrian writer Abu Shama wrote in his chronicle, "Among the amazing things is that the Tartars [=Mongols] were defeated and annihilated by members of

---

[20] Amitai, 58.
[21] Chaliand, 138.

their own race from among the Turks."[22] Abu Shama even composed a poem:

"The Mongols conquered the land and there came to them.

From Egypt a Turk, who sacrificed his life.

In Syria he destroyed and scattered them.

To everything there is a pest of its own kind (jins)."[23]

In the wake of the battle, the Mongol aura of invincibility was also shattered, and the Mamluks acquired prestige and legitimacy for Egypt. By laying waste to Iraq and the Ayyubids in Syria, the Mongols had also inadvertently paved the way for the Mamluks to centralize control of the Islamic world in Cairo. They positioned themselves as the only military that could defend Islam against the foreign invaders, and not one to rest of his laurels, Baybars assassinated the Sultan Qutuz shortly after the battle on a hunting trip and placed himself on the throne, ruling Egypt from 1260-1277. With that, the formerly pagan Turkish slave warriors hailing from the steppes had become the staunchest defenders of Islam, and over the next two centuries, the Mamluk Dynasty in Egypt became the dominant power in the Eastern Mediterranean and champions of the Muslim world.

Cairo became the seat of the Islamic world and the center for scholars, artists, and other educated classes, especially after so many people were forced to flee due to the Mongol invasions in the east. Cairo's prestige and power were reflected in the titles and honorifics bestowed upon the Mamluk sultans: "Pillar of the world and of the faith, Sultan of Islam and of the Muslims, Lord of kings and sultans, Slayer of infidels and polytheists, Supporter of the truth, Helper of mankind, ruler of the two seas, Lord of the qibla and servant of the Holy Places, Reviver of the illustrious caliphate, the Shadow of God on earth, Partner of the Commander of the Faithful, Baybars, son of 'Abd- Allah, the former slave of al-Salih, may God strengthen his authority."[24]

The Mamluk Dynasty continued to practice its policy of isolation from the native population. A military aristocracy, their rule was defined by their aloof nature and separation from both Muslim and non-Muslim subjects under their rule. Mamluk ranks had to be refreshed each generation with a constant stream of fresh slaves from abroad, and to enter the ranks of this isolated military caste, only slaves brought into Cairo having grown up outside of Muslim territory could enter into the service of the sultan or one of the several Mamluk amirs (commanders). The children of these foreign-born warriors were considered free-born Muslims and were thus excluded from the Mamluk system. These offspring were referred to as *awlad al-*

---

[22] Amitai, 58.
[23] Amitai, 59.
[24] Karl Stowasser, *Manners and Customs at the Mamluk Court* (*Muqarnas*, vol. 2, 1984), 13.

nas (sons of respectable people) and fulfilled mostly administrative functions or served as commanders of non-Mamluk troops.[25]

The constant need to replenish ranks was a massive financial and logistical undertaking. Around 2,000 slaves were imported annually into Egypt from various areas on the edges of the Islamic world, including Qipchaq, Azeri and Uzbek Turks, Mongols, Avars, Circassians, Georgians, Armenians, Greeks, Bulgars, Albanians, Serbs, and Hungarians.[26] Inevitably, this ethnic diversity resulted in Mamluk sultans often hailing from different parts of the world. For example, Sultan Lajin (1297-99) hailed from the Baltic area, while the father of Sultan Barquq (1382-89, 1390-99) was a peasant in the Danube region.

A vast network of slave markets eventually became established to serve the Mamluk Dynasty for the purpose of replenishing troops for their empire. Khan Masrur was the main slave market in Cairo, and the city of Alexandria hosted a slave market solely for Mongol slaves. A profitable industry, slave traders from Genoa and Venice competed fiercely against each other as suppliers, with some individual slaves costing up to 100,000 dirhams. Maintenance costs for slaves reached up to 70,000 dirhams a month during the reign of Sultan Al-Nasir Muhammad (1299-1309). The number of slaves owned by a Mamluk amir was a direct reflection of his strength and prestige, and given their importance, bigger numbers helped ensure a ruler's survival during the power struggles that rose up often in the Mamluk system.[27]

Like the earlier Mamluks, the methods of raising these foreign military slaves remained focused on isolation from the native population. The vast majority of slaves came into the Mamluk system at a young age since they were more malleable, and once they were assigned to a barracks, the Mamluk trainees received Islamic religious education provided to them by Muslim clergy (indigenous people mostly of Arabic descent). There were 12 such barracks in the Citadel of Cairo alone, each comprising several buildings with a total of approximatively 1,000 Mamluks. The commander of the Mamluks was known as the *muqaddam al-mamalik*, and the supervisors were palace eunuchs. Mamluks during training received a monthly stipend in addition to food rations and clothing allowances. Discipline remained of utmost importance, and contact with the indigenous population was strictly forbidden for the Mamluk trainees.[28]

---

[25] Although exceptions were sometimes made for the sons of the sultan. This was done to secure a line of succession and achieve stability, allowing the sons to succeed their fathers as the chief Mamluk. This began with Sultan Qala'un al-Alfi (1279-90) until the end of the Bahri Period ("Turkish period") in 1382, before they were overtaken by the Circassian Mamluks, hailing primarily from the Caucasus. Stowasser, 13.

[26] Stowasser, 13.

[27] Stowasser, 14.

[28] Mamluks in training could not leave the Citadel under any circumstances although these restrictions would vary under different sultans. Under Sultan Qala'un, Mamluks were forbidden to leave the Citadel. But these rules were relaxed under Sultan Al-Ashraf Khalil (1290-94), who granted the occasional day trips for his Mamluks. However, restrictions were tightened again by Sultan Al-Nasir Mubammad. Under Al-Nasir, Mamluks were marched to their weekly baths under supervision by supervisory eunuchs. Stowasser, 14.

Once in the sultan's barracks, the young Mamluks were exposed to intense military training. They studied Arabic and the basic tenets of Islam along with training in horsemanship, archery, and other martial arts such as lance, spear, sword, and dagger fighting. These fighting skills were constantly refined and sharpened not only on the barracks training grounds, but also in contests under the watchful eyes of the sultan himself on specially designed practice fields.[29] On these practice fields, Mamluks would showcase their fighting prowess and horsemanship. Sultan Baybars Al-Bunduqdari (1260-77), an excellent archer himself, was a particularly fervent supporter of qabaq contests. Qabaq ("pumpkin" in Turkish) was a game of skill that revolved around a wooden disk-shaped target mounted on a tall pole. Contestants would fire arrows at these targets while lying supine on the back of a horse galloping at full speed. The winners of these contests were given rewards, such as elaborate robes of honor or prized horses.

Once a Mamluk trainee completed his training, he participated in a graduation ceremony called kharj, where he and the rest of the graduating Mamluks would be inspected by the sultan and formally instated into the Royal Mamluk corps. The graduates were given clothing, a horse, a sword, and a posting within the sultan's household.[30]

Intense military discipline resumed among the Mamluks as they entered the palace and continued their military service. The amirs and Mamluks in attendance of the sultan were not allowed to speak to one another.[31] Royal Mamluks needed the sultan's permission to venture on hunting trips or face banishment and other severe punishments. That said, despite these draconian limitations, sultans lavished attention on the well-being of their Mamluks. For example, Sultan Qala'un personally inspected and tasted his Mamluks' food on occasion to ensure it was up to standard.

The Mamluk system was defined by this strict and hierarchical system. Rank, status, appearance, and protocols all defined the Mamluk Dynasty. While it's not unnatural for a military regime to thrive on ceremony and rank, there was another factor to this adherence to discipline. Mamluks hailed from a wide range of ethnic backgrounds and came from vastly different areas of the world, and a military based around this diverse system needed rigid military discipline to compensate for their lack of shared traditions. Many of the Mamluk traditions would evolve into a combination of earlier Islamic practices from Egypt and the previous caliphates, along with Turkish, Caucasian, and even Mongol traditions.

The Wealth of Cairo

By the 13th century, the Mamluk kingdom covered Egypt, Syria, Palestine, southeastern Asia

---

[29] The three practice fields were Midan al-Kabir, located right below the Citadel. Midan al-Qabaq, east of Cairo. Midan al-NaSiri (the area currently occupied by the Tahrir Square) and Midan Siryaqus, located north of Cairo. Stowasser, 14.

[30] Hannah Barker, *Reconnecting with the Homeland: Black Sea Slaves in Mamluk Biographical Dictionaries* (Medieval Prosopography, vol. 30, 2015), 89.

[31] Discipline was so extreme that even glances were forbidden between Mamluks and amirs in the presence of the sultan. Stowasser, 14.

Minor, and the Red Sea rim, and despite the rather rough treatment the Mamluks sometimes dealt the natives of Egypt, the Mamluks still maintained a system of partnership with the educated elite of the Muslim Arab society.[32] The warrior Mamluks needed these educated elites to manage the administrative functions of the kingdom, which included producing a steady flow of taxes from agriculture and trade. It was a symbiotic relationship, with the scholarly classes in Egypt relying on Mamluk military power to protect them against outside threats while they administered the government work and served as judges, scribes, tax collectors, preachers, teachers, hospital administrators, and other non-military functions.[33]

Cairo attracted many of these talented Muslim administrators and educated elite because of the damage dealt throughout the Middle East by the Mongol armies. The Mongol invasions had annihilated Baghdad and Damascus, leaving Cairo as the last major city for Muslim scholars, craftsmen, and merchants. These men took their knowledge and skills to Cairo, propelling the city to great heights.

A medieval depiction of Mongol archers and Mamluk cavalry in battle

The mighty Nile River was of central importance to the city of Cairo. A diverse variety of people sailed on the Nile during the height of Mamluk rule, including merchants, ambassadors,

---

[32] At times, the Mamluks lived up to their steppe warrior origins and dealt out brutal punishments to the natives which included crucifixion and the severing of limbs.
[33] Dunn, 48.

and religious pilgrims from Muslim, Christian, and Jewish backgrounds. Ibn Battuta, a North African historian and traveler, described the sheer mass of people along the banks of Nile: "There is no need for a traveler on the Nile to take any provision with him, because whenever he wishes to descend on the bank he may do so, for ablutions, prayers, purchasing provisions, or any other purpose. There is a continuous series of bazaars from the city of Alexandria to Cairo . . . Cities and villages succeed one another along its banks without interruption and have no equal in the inhabited world, nor is any river known whose basin is so intensively cultivated as that of the Nile. There is no river on earth but it which is called a sea."[34]

While this was certainly a vivid description of the Nile and the nearby market towns, it all paled in comparison to the mighty city of Cairo. The greatest bazaar of its time, travelers visiting the city for the first time were often stunned by its magnificent size. The Italian gentleman Frescobaldi described Cairo on a visit in 1384 as having "a population greater than that of all Tuscany" and "there is a street which has by itself more people than all of Florence."[35] Modern historians estimate that the population of Cairo during the early part of the 14th century was somewhere between 500,000 and 600,000, which was six times larger than Tunis and 15 times larger than London during this period.[36]

There were several reasons Cairo experienced such wealth and prominent growth during the 13th and 14th centuries. First, Cairo was the capital of the Mamluk kingdom, so the entire Turkish ruling class that formed the foundation for Egyptian political and economic life was based there. Second, Cairo is located at a strategic position along the Red Sea to the Nile River spice trading routes and the trading and pilgrimage roads into Africa. Third, the Mamluk armies had successfully defeated the Mongols and saved the Muslim world from being overrun, which ensured that thousands of people fled the destruction of the Mongol invasions and came to Cairo from Syria and Iraq, formerly the most prominent areas of the Islamic caliphate.

The majority of the population of Cairo (called Al-Qahirah, meaning "The Victorious" in Arabic), both the foreign visitors and the natives, lived inside the walls of the city, which was located approximately one and a half miles east of the Nile River. Founded in the 10th century by the Fatimid dynasty as a royal residence and garrison, Cairo eventually evolved as the center of commercial and intellectual life in the region, overtaking Fustat (Misr), an older city located to the south of Cairo. The city was so densely packed that it seemed to border on the edge of overpopulation, and the tide of humanity that resided in the city was overwhelming to many first time visitors.[37] At the same time, the scale of the main avenue was awe inspiring, as thousands of shops were located in the vicinity of the avenue, along with 30 or more markets each focused on a specific trade, including butchers, jewelry dealers, goldsmiths, candle makers, iron workers,

---

[34] Dunn, 45.
[35] Dunn, 45.
[36] Dunn, 45.
[37] Ibn Battuta on his first visit to Bayn al-Qasrayn (the main avenue) was shocked by the sheer volume of people, animals, vendors and markets that packed the streets of Cairo. Dunn, 46.

and slave traders. Like modern cities, Cairo's streets were filled with food vendors, an important part of city life since most citizens lacked proper cooking facilities at home. There was even a large hospital in Cairo built by Sultan Qala'un. Upon seeing the structure, Ibn Battuta was struck by its magnificence and commented that "no description is adequate to its beauties."[38] A modern historian described the hospital: "Cubicles for patients were ranged round two courts, and at the sides of another quadrangle were wards, lecture rooms, library, baths, dispensary, and every necessary appliance of those days of surgical science. There was even music to cheer the sufferers; while readers of the Koran afforded the consolations of the faith. Rich and poor were treated alike, without fees, and sixty orphans were supported and educated in the neighboring school."[39]

Cairo was also filled with colleges, giving the city a vibrant intellectual life. Centered in the madrasas, these mosques were designed for the purpose of teaching rather than prayer. Brought to Cairo from Iraq in the 12th century by Saladin for the purpose of combating the rising Shi'a doctrines of the Fatimid dynasty, the madrasa had become a vital part of life in Cairo, leading Ibn Battuta to note that "as for the madrasas in Cairo, they are too many for anyone to count."[40] Besides curricula on Islamic philosophy and law, studies also included linguistics, medicine, astronomy, and mathematics. Classes were held in halls called liwans.[41]

International trade was crucial in Cairo, and the centers of this commerce were called caravansaries (also funduqs or khans). Located in large and extravagant structures constructed around a courtyard with rooms for storage on the ground floor and upper levels for housing merchants, some caravansaries were built specifically for foreign traders. A particularly large structure built for Syrian merchants in the 12th century had enough lodgings to house up to 4,000 guests at a time.[42]

Mamluk officers were not directly given agricultural estates. Instead, they were granted rights to the revenues generated from the productivity of their lands. Therefore, officers did not usually live on their rural estates and instead chose to live in Cairo. This setup ensured that the revenues from taxes and rents that came from rural areas poured into Cairo and were used for lavish construction projects, producing a renaissance of architecture in the capital. These buildings included palaces, caravansaries, canals, racetracks, and mausoleums. The buildings constructed during this period were increasingly made with stone rather than brick, allowing these structures to last centuries after the fall of the Mamluk Dynasty.

---

[38] Dunn, 50.
[39] Dunn, 50.
[40] Dunn, 50.
[41] Dunn, 50.
[42] Dunn, 46.

The Mamluk "Family"

The Mamluk Dynasty in Egypt would be defined by their disciplined military campaigns against the enemies of Islam and the aloofness they displayed towards the native population they ruled over.[43] Ironically, a Mamluk spent his entire military career defending a population he often disdained, even after he was born a pagan on the steppes in the Eurasian grasslands or in the mountainous regions north and east of the Black Sea. Enslaved as a youth, either the result of capture during combat or sold by his impoverished family, the boy was torn from his native lands and biological kin and thrown into a network of military slavery. The first relationship these youths cultivated was with his slave trader, before being transported to Cairo. Once in Cairo, the youth was then purchased by the sultan, designated for military service, and sent to the barracks in the Cairo Citadel. Besides the sultan, commanders, governors and other high ranking Mamluk officers also purchased their own slaves for their armies.

The entire Mamluk training process was designed to condition these young steppe warriors to be completely loyal to their owners and to their fellow Mamluk trainees, in a sense creating an entirely new family. The purpose was to replace the biological and cultural kinship in their steppe homeland with a new "family," with the owner being the father and fellow Mamluks being brothers.[44] These bonds were particularly intense among those Mamluks who had lived and trained together in the same barracks.

Mamluks in this system was given great prestige and had the capacity to achieve great power for himself, but potential success often depended on the support of his fellow brothers in arms and his current or former owner. It was possible for a Mamluk to climb to great heights in his military or political career, with particularly capable Mamluks becoming commanders, regional governors, or even seizing the sultanate for himself.

The concept of this alienation was supposed to prevent nepotism. Rulers had no incentive to appoint an incompetent relative to positions because they were detached from their biological relatives. Instead, they would rely on their fellow elite Mamluks, all having gone through this system of military training and discipline. In theory, the Mamluk system was designed to provide loyal service without resentment that would be mutually beneficial to both Mamluks and their patrons. As a result, despite being slaves, Mamluks were provided with a first-class education as well as being fully aware that they were part of the ruling class of Egypt. Once freed, they knew that wealth and prestige was possible as they progressed in their careers. In turn, the owners could depend on this trust because their own success directly affected the success of the Mamluks under their command.

This was demonstrated by the names of Mamluks in biographical dictionaries. For a typical

---

[43] So separate were the lives of the Mamluks from the "natives" that the two groups almost never ate together, no matter the rank or station of the individuals. Stowasser, 15.
[44] Barker, 89.

free man, an entry began with his personal name and patronymics (father's name, grandfather's name, etc.). Mamluk entries included only one patronymic: Ibn Abd Allah ("son of a servant of God"). Instead of names rooted in their biological networks, Mamluks received names that referred to their slave traders, owner, and others involved in their slave networks. Thus, there was little incentive for most Mamluks to seek out their original biological kin.[45]

Male Mamluks weren't the only slaves shipped in from abroad. Female slaves from the borders of the caliphate were also brought into the kingdom, mostly imported the same way their counterparts were. However, after this initial importation, the females' experience differed greatly. Like their male counterparts, female Mamluk slaves began their lives as pagans on the Eurasian steppes or mountains and were sold into slavery by their impoverished family, thus losing all contact with her biological network. Upon arrival into Cairo, female Mamluks were subsequently bought by a male owner, who almost always used them for sexual purposes and had them serve as domestic labor or entertainers (such as singers). For a female slave to achieve success, it was imperative that she form an attachment to either a powerful commander or future sultan and bear him children as his wife. Female slaves were comforts and bargaining chips for powerful Mamluks to enjoy or offer up to their partners. Slave women were also owned by civilian men and women, which meant they participated in a wide range of jobs and duties, including hairdressers, bath attendants, nannies, governesses, and even public mourners.

The Royal Mamluk Army

One of the most formidable fighting forces of the time, the Mamluk army had a fearsome reputation. Well-trained and highly professional, they combined the mounted archery of the steppe with the professionalized soldiering skills of the settled empires, and the backbone of this fearsome Mamluk army was the Royal Mamluks.

The Mamluk military was divided into the Royal Mamluks, Mamluks of the amirs, and the troops of the halqa (corps of non-Mamluk cavalry). Within the halqa, there was a special unit that featured the sons of the Mamluks.[46] The Royal Mamluks were given the best military training available, and during the Bahri dynasty (1250-1382), the number of troops in the Royal Mamluks totaled at least 10,000 strong. During the subsequent Circassian dynasty (1382-1517), the numbers for the Royal Mamluks never surpassed this number,[47] but throughout the history of the Mamluk kingdom, the Royal Mamluks formed the bulk of the fighting force and participated in every major military campaign, holding a monopoly on the military and political strength in

---

[45] However, there were exceptions. Sultan Barquq (1382-99) successfully reconnected with his family in the Black Sea region. When Barquq was appointed the commander of the Egyptian army in 1380, he sent for his family in the Caucasus. Summoning his old slave trader, the merchant was able to bring Barquq's father, two cousins and several nephews. Although Barquq's father died shortly after arriving, the other relatives lived very successful lives in Cairo. Even after Barquq left the throne in 1399, the relatives continued to hold high positions of power. Barker, 91.

[46] David Ayalon, *Studies on the Structure of the Mamluk Army--I* (Bulletin of the School of Oriental and African Studies, vol. 15, no. 2, 1953), 204.

[47] Ayalon, 204.

both the Mamluk military and kingdom.

Among the Royal Mamluks, there were two main categories: the Mamluks of the ruling sultan and the Mamluks that passed into the sultan's command from other patrons. Among this latter category, the Royal Mamluks were divided into those who passed into the service of the current sultan from former sultans and Mamluks who entered the current sultan's service from amirs due to the death or dismissal of their patrons.[48] An elite force and the most important regiment of the Mamluk army, the Royal Mamluks were primarily used for frontal attacks. The standard Mamluk formation in battles focused around a battle formation of Royal Mamluks, often led by the sultan himself at the center of the army, with the other Mamluk regiments forming the flanks.[49]

Within the Mamluk institutions (the military, the royal court, and the administrative systems), the ranks were identical. Amirs (commanders) were the central rank of the Mamluk system and were designated by the number of Mamluks under their command.[50] The number of Mamluks under amirs changed constantly. For instance, an amir of 100 could in reality be in charge of 500 Mamluks while also having the title of "Commander of a Thousand." Amirs were well compensated for their positions, and senior amirs could earn an annual tax revenue of 200,000 dinars from their fiefs. Earnings for these fiefs were divided as one-third going straight to the amir, with the rest allocated towards maintaining the Mamluks under his command. The Mamluks in the Royal Court also received generous pay along with the benefits of being under the direct service of the sultan.

Instead of being stationed in garrisons throughout the kingdom, the Royal Mamluks were concentrated in the capital of Cairo. A large unit of Royal Mamluks were located specifically in the barracks at the Citadel, and they only left in large numbers when taking part in an expeditionary military campaign. On rare occasions, some Royal Mamluks were stationed as garrison troops,[51] and as the Mamluks waned in power, the Royal Mamluks began to deploy in smaller numbers in order to quell the constant hotspots that flared in Egypt instead of participating in major military campaigns.

The Royal Mamluks also played a key role in securing power for the sultan. Once a new sultan secured the throne, he immediately tried to uplift his group of Mamluks to power, which was most commonly done via a large and ruthlessly efficient purge of the Mamluks under the previous sultan. Although this brutal purge had been conducted since the emergence of Mamluk rule, it had been a comparatively moderate affair during the Bahri period. This was mostly because the "legitimacy principle" of lineage succession was still functioning at the time and "the young sultan could not regard the mamluks of his father, the preceding ruler, as wholly alien

---

[48] Ayalon, 204.
[49] Chaliand, 139.
[50] Example of amir ranks would be amir of five, of ten, of hundred, etc. Stowasser, 15.
[51] After the conquest of Cyprus, a garrison of Mamluks were deployed to the island. During the Circassian dynasty, a garrison totaling a few dozen Royal Mamluks were also stationed in the holy city of Mecca.

to him, just as his father's mamluks did not consider him a wholly alien sultan."[52]

These purges, while necessary due to the political nature of the Mamluk military, also presented a problem of military leadership. As the new sultan eliminated his rivals from the ranks and supplemented his own ranks with a new generation of young Mamluks, a key deficiency was the lack of experience. By removing these older and more experienced Mamluk officers, the Mamluk army was at risk of losing valuable combat experience, which threatened the army's fighting ability. Therefore, the replacement of the previous officers was done in incremental steps. A common practice by the new sultan was to first appoint his own Mamluks into the lower tiered ranks (amirs of 10, for example) and gradually appoint his Mamluks to the higher ranks over the years.[53]

Over time, however, these purges became more brutal, and some sultans took more drastic steps to secure the loyalty of the Royal Mamluks. Imprisonment and exile were common practices. Sometimes, the young Mamluks under the former sultan were bought by the incoming sultan and incorporated into his cohort, but during the Circassian period (the second half of Mamluk rule in Egypt), flamboyant steps were taken to demonstrate the power of the new sultan.[54] A new sultan's primary concern became a quest to secure control of the Mamluk military as quickly as possible, and there was great uncertainly when it came to this task. The incoming sultan could only rely on his own group of Mamluks, which usually numbered less than 1,000 men and was greatly outnumbered by the Mamluks outside of his direct control. The sultan needed to secure more men that would be loyal to him in the shortest amount of time possible, and since the buying and training of thousands of new, young Mamluks took several years, he needed to weaken the Mamluks under his predecessor as much as possible during the ensuing time gap.[55]

Thus, despite the Mamluk system of military slavery having been established to avoid infighting and inspire loyalty, the Mamluks in Egypt ended up constantly embroiled in extreme infighting and a series of endless coups. This was especially a problem during the latter stages of the Mamluk Dynasty.

Mamluks based the foundations of their identity and careers on the sultan or amir they served, and at the highest level, the Mamluks in the royal court was positioned at the top position in the military hierarchy. However, their fates were interwoven with their sultan, and they only enjoyed this top position as long as their master ruled. If their sultan died, was killed, or deposed, the Mamluks serving in his household and bodyguard fell dramatically in status.[56] This was a very

---

[52] Ayalon, 208.
[53] Ayalon, 208.
[54] The incoming sultan had his Mamluks remove the previous sultan's Mamluks and belongings by force out of the barracks in the Cairo Citadel. Some sultans were even more ruthless. The amirs Mintash and Yalbugha, upon overthrowing Sultan Barquq, almost entirely wiped out the Mamluks under Barquq's command. Ayalon, 209.
[55] Ayalon, 209.
[56] Carl F. Petry, *The Fifteenth Century in the History of Cairo* (The Civilian Elite of Cairo in the Later Middle Ages, 1981), 28.

humiliating demotion of status for proud warriors, and the sudden reversal of fortunes meant that for even the most successful and powerful Mamluks, their positions were constantly at risk.

Additionally, any new sultan viewed the previous Mamluks with suspicion since they were almost surely conspiring to obtain their previous positions. This wasn't excessive paranoia either, because politics in the Mamluk realm revolved around securing one's position with the backing of a loyal group of troops. The ruling sultan was forced to constantly develop and augment his own position to avoid being overthrown and to achieve stability in the kingdom, and during the Bahri dynasty, this system worked. The Bahri Dynasty ruled from 1250 to 1382, and the Bahris were formerly Qipchaqs, a mixed Turkish tribe of Kurds and Mongols hailing from Southern Russia. This was due to a mostly partial system of dynastic succession and the long and stable reigns of the Bahri sultans.

However, during the Circassian period, the second half of Mamluk Egypt, these conditions started to wane. The Circassians originated from the Caucasus. As Mamluk power waned, the political state of the kingdom became increasingly chaotic. Of the 21 Mamluks sultans in the 15th century, only eight of the sultans ruled for more than five years.[57] This constant turnover of power caused a near permanent level of tension that prevailed over the different Mamluk cliques vying for power in the capital, and even the most successful Mamluks could only hope to remain in power for a few years.

On many occasions, new Mamluks had barely entered royal service before their sultan was overthrown, forcing them into an uncertain future. When the new sultan took control, he discharged, imprisoned, or exiled the Mamluks previously in power, and some were tortured or executed to avoid any possibility of rebellion. This ruthless takeover was necessary under this system, as the new sultan needed to surround himself with troops of undying loyalty to him. Any Mamluk who was in the service of the previous ruler was automatically untrustworthy.

The consequences of this constant turmoil and mistrust resulted in a heightened need for new slaves since these new recruits would have no previously held loyalties to any Mamluk sultan or amir. As it turned out, however, the Mamluk kingdom was not as strong economically during the 15th century, so most sultans during this time period couldn't cure the threat of rebellion by importing enough slaves from abroad. This expenditure had always been a major source of the Mamluk military budget and required the kingdom to purchase massive amounts of youth from the eastern steppes, but during the Circassian period, the sultans were both unable and unwilling to buy more than 400-500 new slaves per year.[58]

Compounding matters, this wasn't the only factor in maintaining military readiness. Sultans still had to use revenues to maintain the court and the overall military system while depending on

---

[57] Petry, 21.
[58] Petry, 25.

increasingly shrinking revenues. Due to this, the Circassian sultans could not import enough new Mamluks despite the constant peril of their positions and neglected to reinforce their personal armies with fresh recruits.

To deal with the problems, the sultans started to extort the general population to meet their expenses. Every time a new sultan took control, masses of newly unemployed Mamluks from the previous ruling group were ejected in huge numbers into Cairo, which posed a problem since these deposed Mamluks were essentially a rival military force within the city. During the Circassian period, the sultans responded to this problem in three ways. First, they resorted to simply trying to kill and imprison as many of their rivals as possible, and many out-of-service Mamluks were tortured to death in a brutal fashion. The luckier ones were exiled. In other instances, the sultans resorted to bribery, paying off renegade Mamluks to avoid insurrection. Finally, some sultans simply let these unemployed Mamluks loose into the civilian population,[59] but these masses of unemployed Mamluks were a terror to the native civilians. Having been forcibly removed from service, they were not allowed to receive revenue from the land allotments they had enjoyed while in the service of the sultan, so many of these masterless Mamluks became criminals, robbing and extorting the general population. The sultan was happy to ignore these Mamluks because if they didn't steal from the people, they would likely be asking the ruler for monetary support, but this was a short-sighted policy because these massive groups of vagabond Mamluks remained a constant threat to the ruling sultans. Many of these Mamluks harbored hopes that they could join a successful coup and return to power, and as such, the Circassian sultans were filled with paranoia about this constant internal threat to the empire.

The Fall of the Mamluks

The reputation of the Mamluks as defenders of Sunni Islam against foreign invaders, including the Mongols and the Crusaders, started to add an increasingly heavy burden to the state. It was exceedingly expensive to continue the costs of these military campaigns, and over time, the kingdom started to deteriorate under the rule of Circassian Mamluks.

Native to the Caucasus region near the Black Sea, the Circassian Mamluks had defeated the Bahri Mamluks in the late 14th century and took control of Egypt, but by the 15th century, the costs of these military campaigns were straining the kingdom to the breaking point. For most of the Mamluk Dynasty, the military budget was the central expense of the imperial budget, and during the Circassian period, military campaigns were becoming too expensive for the kingdom to maintain. Given that these expeditions were often unpredictable in terms of length and expense, the costs could not be effectively factored into the budget, and as the royal reserves were depleted, the Mamluks started to extract payments from the civilian population.[60] This caused an enormous strain on the kingdom, one that had been difficult even during the

---

[59] Petry, 28.
[60] Petry, 28.

prosperous times of the kingdom but was exceedingly difficult due to the economically depressed state of the final decades of the Mamluk Dynasty. As agrarian production decreased, so did the revenue that poured into Cairo that supported the Mamluk elite.

Egypt's commerce economy was also weakening during the Circassian period. A major factor for this economic decline was the rapidly changing commercial landscape of the 15th century. From 1450-1550, the state of international trade was experiencing a revolution as European merchants, with the aid of new navigational techniques, were on the hunt for new trade routes. They were motivated by a desire to break the stranglehold Egypt and the Near East had on Europe via their geographical proximity to the lucrative markets of Asia. Previously, the Italian city-states handled the goods transferred from Egypt into Europe, but by the end of the 15th century, Spain, Portugal, and England were actively navigating the seas in hopes of overturning this monopoly, eventually leading the Europeans to their ventures in the Americas. Although the Ottoman Empire was able to resurrect the old trade routes, the Egyptian control of the trade routes in this region would never gain the dominance they enjoyed in the medieval period.[61]

Critically, the Mamluks were not equipped on a fundamental level to adjust to these changing times, and for the most part they lived in blissful ignorance. This was mostly due to the very fabric of Mamluk self-identity and their role in their kingdom - the Mamluks were an isolated military elite who had little respect for the lifestyles and abilities of their subjects. Mamluk training itself fostered a physical separation from the general population, and this enforced a closed circuit in which the Mamluks only emphasized their own values and disregarded all else, an extreme "barracks mentality."[62] The Mamluk rulers were only interested in the economy for their self-interest and only took action to correct problems if their resources were threatened. The state had monopolies on every industry and was supported by a subservient bureaucracy, allowing the Mamluk sultan and amirs to pursue their constant political infightings with no consequences. Thus, as the economic situation worsened over time, the Mamluk rulers were unable to adjust to the kingdom's economic issues and failed to provide the leadership necessary to fix the problems. Instead, they continued to be interested only in furthering their revenue potential.

Another factor was the changing demographics of the steppes. By the end of the 14th century, the supply of young slaves had started to dwindle thanks to Tamerlane, a Turco-Mongol Persianate warlord whose invasions in the east had caused severe demographic changes. These wars forced the Mamluks in Egypt to increasingly fill its ranks with adult Mamluks from other segments of society. According to the historian Maqrizi, these included "sailors, bakery helpers, water carriers, and their ilk."[63] These adult Mamluks were not able or willing to adhere to the strict discipline of the previous generations of Mamluks, so rules had to be relaxed and training

---

[61] Petry, 33.
[62] Petry, 33.
[63] Stowasser, 14.

standards lowered. By 1405, the formerly elite Royal Mamluks had become an impoverished and undisciplined group which Maqrizi described as being "more promiscuous than monkeys" and "more larcenous than mice, more destructive than wolves."[64]

This meant the vaunted Mamluk military was in steep decline as the kingdom decayed. Under the Circassian Mamluks, military discipline reached an all-time low, and when the Circassian Mamluks were defeated by the warlord Tamerlane, the Mamluk military never fully recovered. After that, they slowly lost their edge in military skills, and on top of that, the Mamluks were also slow to adapt firearms and treated gunpowder weapons with contempt. This attitude was not unique at the time, as many warrior castes in Europe and Asia shared this sentiment towards guns, but the Mamluks had the misfortune of being neighbors with the Ottoman Turks, who quickly embraced guns and cannons. The Ottomans incorporated gunpowder into their military as early as 1453, the year they successfully took Constantinople and finished off the Byzantine Empire.

After that, Ottoman Sultan Mehmed II's quest was an attempt to conquer Italy. In Rome, the Pope feared suffering the same fate Constantinople did, so he rallied other Christian states to come to his aid. The Republic of Venice was the only one to refuse out of respect for the peace treaty they had signed with the Ottomans in 1479. Hungary, France, and several other of the Italian city-states replied to the appeal, and in the end, the Ottoman expedition in Italy was short-lived. After conquering Otranto in 1480, they negotiated to give it back to Rome in exchange for free passage while withdrawing from Italy.

Ottoman Sultan Mehmed II died shortly after this endeavour under mysterious circumstances. Out campaigning, showing no signs of weakness or disease, he suddenly fell seriously ill and died within a few days. Some historians claim Mehmed's son and heir, Bayezid II, had poisoned him, while others say it was due to old age and natural causes. Mehmed was in the midst of planning a possible takeover in Egypt when he died, a dream which did not materialize, much to the joy of the Mamluks ruling the southern Mediterranean coast.

In 1514, the Ottomans defeated the Persians, and what made the victory even more decisive was access to artillery, something the Ottomans had acquired under Mehmed II that the Persian Shah repeatedly had refused to do. Ottoman Sultan Selim gained large amounts of land in northern Iraq, northwestern Iran, and present-day Azerbaijan, while the influence of the Shah diminished. He withdrew to his palace, never to be seen on a battlefield again.

After this success, Selim went on to complete his grandfather's dreams of conquering Egypt, currently under the rule of the Mamluks, where, in Cairo, the last Abbasid Caliph sat on the throne. Again, the Ottomans were faced with a traditionally equipped enemy army, proud to use bow and arrow instead of modernizing their armaments. Against the skilled Janissaries equipped

---

[64] Stowasser, 14.

with modern firearms and arquebuses, they didn't stand much of a chance, and Syria was conquered in a single battle. Shortly thereafter, Egypt was defeated after two quick battles, and the Mamluk ruler was exiled to Constantinople.

At that time, the Ottoman Empire was in possession of Damascus, Cairo, and Jerusalem, causing the Arabian Peninsula to fear that the Ottomans were coming for Mecca and Medina. The Sharif of Mecca submitted to Selim without a fight, and with that the holiest cities of Islam had fallen into his hands easier than could have been anticipated. This was a significant conquest, as it shifted the center of the empire from the old Byzantine past toward important Arabic Islamic strongholds. Selim was graced with the humble title of "The Servant of the Two Holy Cities", and today it is debated whether or not the exiled Caliph transferred his title to Selim, as historians from the 17th century had claimed. Since Selim did not exercise any sacred rights following his possible elevation, modern historians conclude this was not the case.

Selim's reign lasted only eight years, but his legacy was of great importance to what would come with Suleiman the Magnificent, the next ruler. The eight years of conquest expanded the area of the Ottoman Empire by 70%, an expansion made possible thanks to the Ottomans' interest in science and modernisation. The acquisition of superior armaments and weapons proved pivotal in battles with the traditionally equipped Safavid and Mamluk armies, whereas the modernization of the Ottoman armies had started since the conquest of Constantinople under the lead of Mehmed II some 60 years earlier. The Janissaries had developed into a very strong and forceful nucleus, which played a major part in Selim's successful conquests. Together with the fiscal and political apparatus improved under Bayezid II, the Ottoman Empire became a world force, ready to take the lead in political, economic, cultural, and military arenas in and outside their territory. All of this paved the way for the real apogee of the Ottoman Empire under the rule of Selim's successor, Suleiman the Magnificent.

Although the Mamluks were technically removed from power in Egypt by the Ottomans, they remained an influential part of society there. Egypt proved to be a vital appendage of the Ottoman Empire, as a trade center linking India with the Mediterranean and as a producer of grain. It became a crucial component of Ottoman existence, and the slave soldiers were thoroughly subordinated to Ottoman rule. Their role as rulers and leaders was usurped, but nonetheless, they were retained as the military basis of Egypt, the newest province of the Ottoman Empire. Seven Mamluk regiments were founded, consisting of five cavalry and two infantry units. The military establishment was staffed and commanded by Ottoman loyalists, comprising usually Anatolian Turks, Bosnians, Albanians, converted Jews, Armenians, Georgians and Circassians, bonded by the loyalties of empire, and mastery of the Ottoman language, which was an aristocratic, Persian modulated form of Turkish.

In respect of Ottoman rule, a viceroy or governor was present in Egypt, and initially, rule was direct from Constantinople and powerfully centralized. However, by the time Napoleon's army landed in Egypt, the authority of the Ottoman viceroy was titular, and power had been usurped once again by the Mamluks. Egypt lay under the control of two Mamluk chieftains, Ibrahim Bey and Murad Bey. Of the two, it is Ibrahim Bey who is listed by most encyclopedias as Egyptian ruler of the period, although not as an appointee of the Sublime Porte. When their owner, Mehmet Ebu Zahab, died on campaign in 1775, Ibrahim and Murad established themselves as the paramount Beys of Egypt, consigning the Ottoman viceroys to a subordinate position. The two were of Georgian origin, and thus the Georgians became paramount in Egypt, retaining strong ties to their homeland, which, as Russia expanded into the Caucuses, lay increasingly within the sphere of influence of St. Petersburg. Russian alliances were explored, and it became likely that Russia would establish some degree of control over the region. Facing the difficulty of recruiting enough Mamluks locally to maintain the purity of the military elite, a brigade of five hundred Russian troops were introduced into Egypt in 1786. This was all in the way of setting the tone for things to come.

A French portrait of Murad Bey

The two powerful Beys were not by any means united, and throughout their shared power, they were consistently engaged in a war of intrigue and political maneuver that from time to time broke out into violence. Officially, the Mamluk army in Egypt comprised 60,000 men at arms, in a position to take to the field at any time. This was certainly not the case, and notwithstanding spirited adherence to military culture, there were in fact only about 6,000 mounted and ready Mamluks ready when Napoleon and the French invaded Egypt at the end of the 18th century. These were aided in battle by Bedouin levies of wildly fluctuating numbers although the Bedouins were apt always to back the winning side, and to switch sides if the tide seemed to be shifting. They were, as a consequence, loyal only to their own interests, and fought on behalf of, or turned against any at any time.

When Napoleon entered Alexandria, the Mamluks retreated, the Bedouin switched sides, and the citizen militias melted away. Ibrahim Bey and Murad Bey then consolidated their forces and met in Cairo to consider their response to this invasion. As warriors, their solution to the problem was war, and despite the improbable odds of victory, they were determined that they would fight.

Meanwhile, as his army was disembarked and reorganized, Napoleon also began to consider his next move. He was not particularly impressed with Alexandria, which did not to his mind live up to its mythic origins, or its reputation. Nonetheless, in Alexandria he began to establish the rhetorical terms under which he would govern. These terms were rhetorical only because they were political, and not necessarily to be trusted, but they were nonetheless shrewd. In an effort to identify with the Islamic majority of the country, Napoleon claimed that the French were "Muslim" insofar as they were unitarian, and venerated the "One God," attaching no particular importance to mothers, sons and trinities as the Catholics did. What he meant by that is somewhat lost in translation, but nonetheless, he recognized the power of religion in Egypt, and if he had no particular intention of using it, then he certainly wished to avoid antagonizing it. As he put it, "If I governed Jews, I would raise the Temple of Solomon."

He was also careful to identify local hierarchies, and to place them under his control, interfering as little as possible with the traditional chain of command, but simply subordinating it to a French upper hierarchy, headed by himself. French identity was demanded in sashes and cockades, other items of uniform, and the tricolour was prominently displayed throughout the city.

Finally, notwithstanding lavish promises to liberate the people from their rapacious masters of yore, a heavy tribute was imposed on the population. The Egyptians, like most conquered peoples, would pay for their own conquest, or liberation, as the French propaganda had it.

As the French took over, the Mamluk hierarchy gathered in Cairo, certain that the most awful fate awaited the city at the moment the French overpowered its defenses. An urgent message was sent to the Turkish Sultan via the Ottoman Viceroy to Egypt, a figurehead acting as a messenger of the Beys. Help was urgently requested, although, in real terms, neither the Egyptian rulers nor Napoleon anticipated that the Ottoman Empire would be willing to clash swords with France. Of course, loud and strident diplomatic protests were heard from Constantinople, but beyond that, the Sublime Porte was content to sit on its hands. The Ottoman-Egyptians, in practical terms the two Beys and their Mamluk supporters, were on their own.

The Mamluks represented a military culture with a proud and ancient tradition, and they certainly had no intention of folding in the face of an infidel invasion. Recognizing the inevitable fact that Napoleon would advance on Cairo, it was decided that an army would be raised. There was, initially at least, great confidence among the Mamluk elite that the French would be defeated. The Mamluks fought primarily as cavalry, with infantry as a secondary resource. A highly mobile cavalry provided a strike force ideally suited to the terrain upon which this war would be fought. The French arrived on foot, largely without horses, and Napoleon's expectation that horses would be easily acquired in Egypt had proved unfounded. The French would fight a foot infantry war, and the Mamluks could think of no practical reason why they would not be slaughtered in the desert.

Napoleon had two reasons to waste no time in advancing on Cairo. The first was simply that he wished to deny the Beys the opportunity to prepare their defenses, but also he realized that Nelson would at some point appear with the British fleet, and he wished to be in command of the whole country before that happened. On July 5, leaving just 2,000 troops to garrison Alexandria, Napoleon set off with the balance of his army towards Cairo. Two columns set off directly across the desert, while a third moved along the coast to take the port city of Rosetta, after which it would divert south to link up with the main divisions.

The folly, or perhaps, as Napoleon saw it, the necessity of striking out into the Egyptian desert at the beginning of July 1798 made itself felt very quickly. In an effort to retain the secret of where the expedition was headed, Napoleon had ordered that no water canteens be issued, and they were not. Now, in the punishing head of the North African summer, French troops, dressed in flannels and boots began to drop like flies from dehydration and heat exhaustion. By July 8, the port of Rosetta was taken, and the French column assigned to that task was somewhat replenished. Amid the happier circumstances of marching down the west bank of a Nile tributary, it set off southwards to link up with the main French force.

On July 12, Napoleon passed in review of his troops and delivered a speech warning that hardships yet remained, and that a battle remained to be fought before Cairo. There he promised his men that "we will have all of the bread we want."

That evening, the army was on the move again, this time heading inland to the settlement of Shubra Khit, a few miles downriver from Rahmaniya, and it was there that they caught sight for the first time some of Murad Bey's cavalry. For most French soldiers, this was their first sight of a Mamluk cavalryman, magnificent and medieval. The Mamluk were supremely confident, resplendent as they were in armor, wielding fine, but obsolete weapons and mounted on their fast Arab horses. By comparison, the French, threadbare and exhausted, many soldiers with no buttons on their tunics after having found them to be an excellent currency, seemed defeated already.

The battle that followed was relatively minor, and it was by way of testing French defenses. To the surprise of the Mamluk commanders, it revealed an obvious truth. For all of their abstract magnificence, and their familiarity with the battlefield, tactics would win the day. As the Mamluks mobilized and commenced a charge, the French promptly formed up into squares, a disciplined maneuver and by then a standard European infantry response to a cavalry attack. In essence, an infantry square comprised a division, its ranks between six and eight deep, formed up into a square or a rectangle, with artillery, cavalry and baggage in the center and guns deployed at each corner.

If the open desert was the terrain upon which the Mamluk cavalry had been born, it was no less ideal for the infantry square. Mamluk cavalrymen surged forward, and waiting until they could see the whites of their eyes, the French infantrymen, their Charleville Model 1777 muskets more accurate than anything the Mamluk had ever before seen, opened fire. For an hour, the Mamluk cavalry charged the squares, and time and again they were beaten back with heavy losses. In the meanwhile, three French gunboats on the river added to the carnage, engaging a small Egyptian flotilla that came out to engage. As the attack showed signs of faltering, Napoleon ordered his troops on the offensive, relieving the French gunboats and driving the Mamluks back 100 miles to the town of Embabeh, on the southern outskirts of Cairo, where they regrouped and waited.

The Battle of Shubra Khit was an inconsequential, opening engagement that was no more than enough to burst the early confidence of the Mamluks. Only some 12,000, or perhaps 13,000 Mamluks were present at the battle, and with only 6,000 of their number mounted. Accustomed to overwhelming the untrained infantry of Egyptian villages with their spectacular displays and virtuoso horsemanship, the Mamluk cavalry was shocked at the outcome. This was something entirely different. A modern, professional and trained army of disciplined soldiers was not easy to intimidate or overwhelm.

For their part, the French were still impressed with the conduct of the enemy despite their shattering defeat. It was not typically part of the Gallic temper to compliment or pay tribute to an enemy, but even as they were shooting them down, French soldiers marveled at the sheer élan of these magnificently attired warriors from another age, riding to their deaths with almost suicidal disdain. Their horsemanship and their ability to fight on horseback mesmerized the French, but what they lacked was simply a cogent strategy to deal with the simple mechanics of a square. The effect of it must have been similar to the historic ancestors of the French, the Gauls, when meeting the Roman legions for the first time. Without a radical reevaluation of tactics, defeat would be inevitable, and yet, the mindset of both soldiers and commanders remained frozen in another time. The Mamluks, waiting for Napoleon to catch up with them, were preparing an almost identical battlefield.

As the Mamluks fled south, and prepared a stand, local Egyptian villages, for whom the writing was now clearly on the wall, began to seek an accommodation with the French. Clearly, the wider population was adjusting to the reality that the Nile Valley had been conquered. Napoleon pressed on in pursuit of the retreating Ottoman-Egyptians, bearing down relentlessly on Cairo. Once again, the army marched forward in square formation, six ranks deep, the artillery contained within. After the horrors of the desert crossing, the sharp victory energized the French army and made the soldiers confident. Napoleon promised everything to everybody once Cairo was reached, and a sense of denouement gripped the troops as they bore down on the ultimate battle.

The scene, despite its heroic depictions in the art of the campaign, which Napoleon fastidiously commissioned as a steady output of propaganda, was not pretty. Napoleon required as much as possible that his soldiers live off the land, and the commissariat of the entire expedition seemed to have failed or been misdirected. The lack of canteens for the simple purpose of carrying water was an obvious, rather unforgivable oversight under the circumstances, but there were many other complaints too. The hardtack biscuits, for example, issued to the troops as campaign rations, were spoiled, and so food was scarce. An undisciplined pillage of the countryside resulted as the army marched through the countryside. Most of the infantry was by then dressed in the rags of uniforms, their brass buttons often cut off and exchanged for food. Napoleon himself subsisted on boiled lentils and sour biscuits, reading the signs as discipline began to crumble. He later wrote in his memoirs, "[T]he evil was in the ferment of the mind." Numerous incidences of men refusing to obey orders were recorded, and discipline was harsh and arbitrary.

In the end, Napoleon maintained control largely through the application of harsh discipline, backed up by inspirational exhortations. "Courage on the field of battle is insufficient to make a good soldier," he said. "It requires, as well, the courage to face fatigue and privation. Suppose I had the intention of journeying to Asia after the conquest of Egypt? To march in the traces of Alexander, I would need to have his soldiers."

As the French approached the outlying settlements, the citizens of Cairo met to make final preparations. Upon discussion between Ibrahim Bey, Murad Bey, the Ottoman viceroy and other dignified townsmen, it was decided that a stand would be made at the riverine port of Bulaq. Ibrahim Bey would place his forces on the east bank of the Nile and Murad Bey would position his fortifications at Embabeh, on the west bank. There, on July 21, 1798, the Battle of Embabeh was fought.

For all of its historic significance, the Battle of Embabeh, or the Battle of the Pyramids, as it was ultimately named, was short and entirely one-sided. After his experience at the Battle of

Shubra Khit, Napoleon realized that the only fighting men of any value in the opposing army were the Mamluk cavalry, and again, it was the simple strategy of forming infantry squares that suggested itself to him. Gathering his troops in preparation to fight, Napoleon, at least according to the popular version of the story, pointed to the Pyramids, obscured by the haze, and declared that 40 centuries of history would be looking down on the events of that day.

He would have had to squint to see the Pyramids, half lying half buried in sand some 15 miles away to the south. Nonetheless, it was thus that the battle was reported to the Directory, and obviously not content with an anonymous Egyptian village as the site of his great victory, Napoleon extrapolated the facts somewhat by naming the engagement the Battle of the Pyramids. This sat a great deal more majestically in the pages of history, and the battle itself has somewhat tended to reflect the glory of its superb name.

A little after noon on July 21, 1798, Napoleon formed up his troops and ordered them into squares. Five divisions did as they were ordered, and as usual the baggage, artillery and cavalry was held in the protected center. By 14h00, his army was advancing against Murad Bey's positions, the right flank leading and the left flank protected by the Nile.

Murad fixed his right flank at the Nile, at the village known as Embabeh, which was fortified and held by infantry comprising mainly Egyptian levies and Bedouin irregulars, supported by vintage cannons fixed in position, and unable to swivel or aim. Murad's cavalry, the pivot upon which his army fought, deployed in the open desert on the left flank. The two armies faced one another north to south. On the east bank, Ibrahim Bey watched, but, separated by the river, he was unable to offer assistance.

Napoleon stood poised at the head of an army of 25,000 men, not perhaps in a peak of condition, but battle-ready and seasoned, and locked in a simple strategy that had very little chance of failure. Facing him was a force of some 15,000 infantry, neither trained nor configured to confront the French, leaving the field to the 6,000 or so cavalry. At about 15h30, the Mamluk cavalry, without warning, launched itself into action, and in a virtual repeat of the Battle of Shubra Khit, waves of attacking horsemen broke against the walls of infantry. The picture painted by numerous canvases, and acres of commemorative prose, describes the squares, immovable and impenetrable, surrounded by galloping horsemen, searching for an opportunity to attack, but in their inevitable defeat, displaying the last of their obsolete brilliance.

Once expended the Mamluk cavalry broke and pulled back, and immediately Napoleon ordered his troops forward to deal with the enemy infantry. As they watched the cavalry decimated, many of the infantry melted away, but those who remained were trapped against the Nile. There they were ruthlessly slaughtered, with many leaping into the Nile in an attempt to get to the other side. Hundreds drowned, and many were picked off by crocodiles.

French casualty figures place their own losses at just 29, with Ottoman-Egyptian losses running into many thousands, most crucially among them some 3,000 cavalry, a little under half of those deployed in the field. It was a devastating defeat for the army of Murad Bey, but an easy and well-fought victory for the French. The army of Ibrahim Bey, watching in dismay at the ease with which the larger half of Egypt's defense was broken, quickly dispersed. News of the defeat was not long in reaching Cairo, and realizing that this round at least was lost, the Mamluks gathered their households and their treasure and decamped the city. Murad Bey headed south, and Ibrahim Bey went east. Many set off across the Sinai into Syria, and others pushed further south, deep in the desert of the Upper Nile.

A French artist's painting depicting the battle

Napoleon in Cairo, by Jean-Léon Gérôme

The departure of the Mamluk leadership plunged the delta region of the Nile, the most populous quarter of Egypt, into chaos. Bedouins began looting, and as law and order began to break down, populations turned on one another. Even as the French army marched along the Nile to Cairo, they continued to encounter sporadic resistance. Most bothersome were the ongoing predations of the Bedouin, picking off stragglers and looting and stealing what they could find.

There was no conspicuous welcome offered the invading troops in the streets of the capital, and certainly no high-minded rhetoric of freedom and liberation impressed upon a population determined to put up resistance wherever it could. Napoleon sent envoys ahead to Cairo to reassure the ruling and mercantile classes that the French did not intend to loot the city or slaughter its inhabitants. Thanks to this, the exodus from Cairo did slow somewhat, but sensing that speech and action did not always meet, much of the wealth of the city was loaded onto camels and donkeys and shipped out anyway. Ironically, waiting at the edges of the city, and on the roads and highways east and south, were the Bedouin tribesmen, ready to avail themselves of the prevailing lawlessness to strip every caravan of its valuables.

Ibrahim Bey's mansion near Cairo

Despite this, the French army fought a well-disciplined rearguard action all the way into Cairo, and even there, hostility was palpable. The French took up the residences of the departed Beys, and in some instances their wives and daughters, but their treasure that Napoleon had so anticipated had been largely removed. Ibrahim Bey had retreated to the adjacent Sharqiya Province, with its capital at Bilbeis, and with him he had Ebu Bekir Pasha, the Ottoman viceroy of Egypt and a symbol of sovereignty and legitimacy for many Egyptians.

Napoleon might have been in occupation of Cairo, but he was a long way from claiming conquest of Egypt. Behind him lay the vast deserts of Libya, and ahead Syria, an Ottoman territory extending in the late 18th century to the Sinai. This offered Ibrahim Bey strategic depth and support while limiting Napoleon's scope of maneuver. To pacify Ibrahim by force, Napoleon would need to ride into the desert, an endless expanse into which Ibrahim Bey and his men could easily retreat. The Ottoman ruler of Acre, Ahmed Cezzar Pasha, might also take the opportunity to come to Ibrahim's aid.

Among the first issues that Napoleon had to consider were force levels and security. So long as the Royal Navy maintained its blockade of Egyptian ports, no French troopship would dare attempt to land. At the same time, the difficulties of climate and disease had critically reduced the original size of the French force, to the point that Napoleon began to contemplate the recruitment of young Egyptians. Although the policy did not have much time to mature and was never fully implemented, Napoleon issued orders that all young Mamluks, those more than 8 years old and under 16, all boys abandoned in Cairo, and those who had once been slaves, would be incorporated into the demi-brigades, either as soldiers or drummers.[65]

---

[65] A *demi-brigade* is a French military formation, meaning a half-brigade, incorporating various infantry units, and commanded by a *chef de brigade*.

This has held up as the beginnings of French universalism in regards to its subject peoples overseas, and possibly this was so, for the French would certainly extend this policy to the African colonies as they were accumulated. The French concept of assimilation was simply that foreign subjects, no matter how exotic, could, given the right exposure, emerge as liberated, republican Frenchmen. This simple, yet idealistic concept, one that would underwrite the early French colonial experience in Africa, had its genesis in Egypt.

Napoleon's next priority was to deal with the discord rife at the senior command level. He invited a number his top commanders to dinner one night, and when dinner was over, he inquired of each how he was doing in Egypt. The response was generally enthusiastic and positive, to which Napoleon expressed his satisfaction. "I know that many generals are fostering mutinies and preaching revolt," he said. "They should take care. The distance of a general and of a drummer boy to me is the same, and if the occasion presents itself, I will have the one shot as easily as the other."

The next problem was probably the most pressing, and that was the pacification of Egypt itself. Napoleon simply did not have the force to garrison and control the populated Nile Delta, let alone the vast and sparsely populated hinterland. Resistance to French rule was increasingly manifest in a complete lack of security for any Frenchman, or any collaborator, anywhere in the country.

The question was simply one of legitimacy. Conquest, of course, offers the simple legitimacy of "might is right," and that certainly paved the way for the Ottoman rule of Egypt, but that did not and could not extend to a European power of Catholic origins. The belief and expectation that Napoleon intended to outlaw Islam and replace it with Christianity was impossible to dislodge. The only solution, then, was to more closely identify Napoleon and his new regime with Islam, in the hope that he would be accepted as a legitimate liberator. According to historian Juan Cole, author of *Napoleon's Egypt: Invading the Middle East*, "Bonaparte felt that the chief obstacle to the acceptance of French authority in Egypt would be Islam and that only a government of the clerics could plausibly lend their authority to his contention that French deists were as acceptable as Muslims when it came to rule."[66]

Napoleon tried to frame his invasion as liberation from rule by the Mamluks and Ottomans, attempting in this way to differentiate between "us and them," and thus increasingly seemed to have a Muslim complexion. On July 27, 1798, he formed an advisory council, a "Divan," comprising eminent, local, Muslim scholars, theologians and clergymen. Tradesmen and merchants, and eminent men of secular positions were not included. Napoleon was working to cultivate an Islamophilic public image, albeit doing so rather transparently, and the polarity of his Divan never suggested any real authority.

---

[66] Cole, Juan. *Napoleon's Egypt: Invading the Middle East.* (Palgrave Macmillan, New York, 2007) p75

Napoleon registered fairly quickly that promising the Egyptians "liberty," in the French, republican sense of the word, was pointless since all things tended to revolve around religion. The idea of liberty from the demands of religion, and the control of religious leaders, was absurd, and it bore no fruit whatsoever. Clearly, the identity of the revolution would need to be modified, and that modification would require the French to adapt to Islamic religious peculiarities, and not vice versa.

If it wasn't already, it would become clear in the coming months that Napoleon had bitten off more than he could chew, and he would suffer reversals while pushing into the Middle East from Egypt. By 1801, the French were out of power in Egypt, replaced for the most part by the British. Initially, the British maintained a strong presence in Egypt to separate the Mamluk and Ottoman forces, not only to keep the peace, but also to ensure that the French did not attempt to retake the territory. In reality, the early 19th century marked the moment of British predominance in Egypt, a presence that would survive through the end of World War II.

Online Resources

Other books about Middle East history by Charles River Editors

Other books about the Mamluks on Amazon

Bibliography

Amitai, Reuven. "The Mamlūk Institution, or One Thousand Years of Military Slavery in the Islamic World." *Arming Slaves: From Classical Times to the Modern Age*, edited by CHRISTOPHER LESLIE BROWN and PHILIP D. MORGAN, Yale University Press, New Haven; London, 2006, pp. 40–78.

Ayalon, David. "The Mamlūks of the Seljuks: Islam's Military Might at the Crossroads." *Journal of the Royal Asiatic Society*, vol. 6, no. 3, 1996, pp. 305–333.

Ayalon, David. "Studies on the Structure of the Mamluk Army --I." *Bulletin of the School of Oriental and African Studies, University of London*, vol. 15, no. 2, 1953, pp. 203–228.

Ayalon, David. "The System of Payment in Mamluk Military Society." *Journal of the Economic and Social History of the Orient*, vol. 1, no. 1, 1957, pp. 37–65.

Ayalon, David. "The End of the Mamlūk Sultanate: (Why Did the Ottomans Spare the Mamlūks of Egypt and Wipe out the Mamlūks of Syria?)." *Studia Islamica*, no. 65, 1987, pp. 125–148.

Barker, Hannah. "Reconnecting with the Homeland: Black Sea Slaves in Mamluk Biographical Dictionaries." *Medieval Prosopography*, vol. 30, 2015, pp. 87–104.

Berkey, Jonathan. "'Silver Threads among the Coal': A Well-Educated Mamluk of the Ninth/15th century." *Studia Islamica*, no. 73, 1991, pp. 109–125.

Black, Antony. "Mamluk Ideology and the Sultan-Caliph." *The History of Islamic Political Thought: From the Prophet to the Present*, NED - New edition, 2 ed., Edinburgh University Press, Edinburgh, 2011, pp. 145–148.

Chaliand, Gérard. "The Seljuks, the Mamluks, and the Crusades." *A Global History of War: From Assyria to the Twenty-First Century*, et al., 1st ed., University of California Press, 2014, pp. 127–140.

Crecelius, Daniel, and Gotcha Djaparidze. "Relations of the Georgian Mamluks of Egypt with Their Homeland in the Last Decades of the Eighteenth Century." *Journal of the Economic and Social History of the Orient*, vol. 45, no. 3, 2002, pp. 320–341.

Dunn, E. Ross. "The Mamluks." *The Adventures of Ibn Battuta: A Muslim Traveler of the Fourteenth Century*, 3rd ed., University of California Press, 2012, pp. 41–64.

Fay, Mary Ann. "Egypt in the Eighteenth Century: The Transition from the Medieval to the Early Modern." In *Unveiling the Harem: Elite Women and the Paradox of Seclusion in Eighteenth-Century Cairo*, Syracuse, New York: Syracuse University Press, 2012, pp. 45-66.

Galor, Katharina and Bloedhorn Hanswulf. "The Mamluk Period." *The Archaeology of Jerusalem: From the Origins to the Ottomans*, Yale University Press, 2013, pp. 209–231.

Levanoni, Amalia. "The Mamluk Conception of the Sultanate." *International Journal of Middle East Studies*, vol. 26, no. 3, 1994, pp. 373–392.

Levanoni, Amalia. "The Mamluks' Ascent to Power in Egypt." *Studia Islamica*, no. 72, 1990, pp. 121–144.

Meloy, John L. "Imperial Strategy and Political Exigency: The Red Sea Spice Trade and the Mamluk Sultanate in the 15th century." *Journal of the American Oriental Society*, vol. 123, no. 1, 2003, pp. 1–19.

Petry, Carl F. "The 15th century in the History of Cairo." In *The Civilian Elite of Cairo in the Later Middle Ages*, Princeton University Press, 1981, pp.15-36.

Poliak, A. N. "Some Notes on the Feudal System of the Mamlūks." *Journal of the Royal Asiatic Society of Great Britain and Ireland*, no. 1, 1937, pp. 97–107.

Stowasser, Karl. "Manners and Customs at the Mamluk Court." *Muqarnas*, vol. 2, 1984, pp. 13–20.

Tor, D.G. "The Mamluks in the Military of the Pre-Seljuq Persianate Dynasties." *Iran*, vol. 46, 2008, pp. 213–225.

Van Steenbergen, Jo. "The Mamluk Sultanate as a Military Patronage State: Household Politics and the Case of the Qalāwūnid Bayt (1279-1382)." *Journal of the Economic and Social History of the Orient*, vol. 56, no. 2, 2013, pp. 189–217.

Wolff, Anne. "The Mamluk Rulers of Egypt." *How Many Miles to Babylon?: Travels and Adventures to Egypt and Beyond, From 1300 to 1640*, 1st ed., Liverpool University Press, 2003, pp. 14–39.

Free Books by Charles River Editors

We have brand new titles available for free most days of the week. To see which of our titles are currently free, click on this link.

Discounted Books by Charles River Editors

We have titles at a discount price of just 99 cents everyday. To see which of our titles are currently 99 cents, click on this link.

Made in the USA
Monee, IL
20 March 2023